For years I
followed you
like a tail, and
on happy days,
I wagged.

I will be you
when I have
what you have.

THE BOOK OF EVERYDAY INSTRUCTION

CHLOË BASS

THE OPERATING SYSTEM C. 2018

```
the operating system
print//document
```

THE BOOK OF EVERYDAY INSTRUCTION

ISBN: 978-1-946031-37-2
Library of Congress Control Number: 2018939195
copyright © 2018 by Chloë Bass
edited and designed by ELÆ [Lynne DeSilva-Johnson]
assistant copyeditor: D. Allen

For additional questions regarding reproduction, quotation, or to request a pdf for review contact operator@theoperatingsystem.org

This text was set in Impact Label, Helvetica Neue, Courier, Minion, and OCR-A Standard, printed and bound by Spencer Printing, in Honesdale, PA, in the USA. Books from The Operating System are distributed to the trade by SPD/Small Press Distribution, with ePub and POD via Ingram.

2018-19 OS System Operators
CREATIVE DIRECTOR/FOUNDER/MANAGING EDITOR: ELÆ [Lynne DeSilva-Johnson]
DEPUTY EDITOR: Peter Milne Greiner
CONTRIBUTING EDITORS: Kenning JP Garcia, Adrian Silbernagel, Amanda Glassman
UNSILENCED TEXTS ASSISTANT EDITOR/TRANSLATOR: Ashkan Eslami Fard
SERIES COORDINATOR, DIGITAL CHAPBOOKS: Robert Balun
JOURNEYHUMAN / SYSTEMS APPRENTICE: Anna Winham
SOCIAL SYSTEMS / HEALING TECH: Curtis Emery
VOLUNTEERS and/or ADVISORS: Adra Raine, Alexis Quinlan, Clarinda Mac Low, Bill Considine, Careen Shannon, Joanna C. Valente, Michael Flatt, L. Ann Wheeler, Jacq Greyja, D. Allen, Charlie Stern, Joe Cosmo Cogen, Sarah Dougherty, Bahaar Ahsan, you

The operating system is a member of the Radical Open Access Collective, a community of scholar-led, not-for-profit presses, journals and other open access projects. Now consisting of 40 members, we promote a progressive vision for open publishing in the humanities and social sciences. Learn more at: http://radicaloa.disruptivemedia.org.uk/about/

Your donation makes our publications, platform and programs possible!
We <3 You. http://www.theoperatingsystem.org/subscribe-join/

```
the operating system
```
Brooklyn, New York
www.theoperatingsystem.org

THE BOOK OF EVERYDAY INSTRUCTION

For all the people we invent.
For you (and me).

The Book of Everyday Instruction is an eight-chapter
project exploring one-on-one social interaction —
in other words, pairing. In a search through my
inbox to find something else about the early days of
this work, I discovered that I had referenced it as
an "autistic cookbook project" as early as 2013. At
that time, I had just finished *The Bureau of Self-
Recognition*, which studied intimacy at the scale of
the self. I knew that this work was the next step
without being able to anticipate what it would, or
could be. As the *Bureau* helped me through a difficult
period of understanding myself, I hoped that the
Book could be a similar guide to connecting me with
others, one person at a time.

It took me two years to return to the gist of the
project. (The reasons for that are simultaneously
complex and uninteresting, like much of our internal
lives.) Upon return, I found that there were a few
questions I was genuinely pondering about what it
means to be with another person. The first, how do we
know when we're really together? became the backdrop
for chapter one. Everything else, I'd like to say,
followed, but it is more truthful to say that it
expanded. From seemingly simple interactions and
live experiences, to permanent public installations,
to experimentation with smartphone apps; from a
single person to a concept of partnership between a
person and a city, the work unfolded in surprising
directions motivated by the false clarity inspired
by the question format (a question implies that
there might be, somewhere, an answer).

What happens with a project that takes too many
shapes to count is that it begins to feel more
and more like life. Each chapter relied on all of
its elements in order to function, whether or not

it's possible to make everything visible in either exhibition or book format. It is my hope to share the interplay between artistic output that could easily be captured in still images and that which could not. There are moments of the work that are always missing: past experiences that you didn't have, or souvenirs for memories in the future that haven't been made yet. No matter how much I add to this book, it will never be enough.

Although my work focuses only very partially on the details of my own private life, each of my intimacy investigations is, for me, a form of healing and discovery. Over the course of making *The Book of Everyday Instruction*, I meant for myself to fall in love — in the romantic way, the one that relates to partnership, and to home. I believed that this project could be specifically and personally healing, but I had a limited scope of what "well" might mean. In fact I did fall in love, many times, in ways I could not have predicted or expected.

The premise of this work — and indeed of most of my projects — is that you could do it yourself. I have stated clearly, although not without some grandiosity, that a goal of my work is to get us to live better together. Let this book serve as an invitation not necessarily to follow the steps of my projects to the letter (too much has been left out for that), but to feel something that reminds you of your own life and relationships. I leave this document as some intersection of past record, and future souvenir.

In the end, this is all about you.

CHLOË BASS
Brooklyn, NY
2018

Every Thursday morning for eight weeks I brought flowers to *The Book of Everyday Instruction*. I found the vases in the galleries that contained wilting flowers, removed them, exchanged the wilting flowers for fresh ones, and returned them to their given places beneath or alongside artworks and architectural features such as ledges and wooden beams. They were unassuming flowers. Some were yellow or white daisies; others looked like wildflowers, the kind you might find on the side of the road in a more rural location than Queens, New York.

The flowers came to Chloë and me as we installed *The Book of Everyday Instruction*. When we began installing the show at Knockdown Center, there were a handful of small brown bottles filled with daffodils that had been left over from a conference the weekend prior. We distributed the flowers throughout the exhibition as a festive element for the opening reception and quickly decided that it made sense for them to remain as part of the installation: a shared gesture that resides somewhere between curatorial and artistic authorship, analogous to the way in which authorship of Chloë's work is shared between herself and her participants. I, as curator and institutional caretaker, happily took on the responsibility of replacing the flowers weekly for the duration of the exhibition.

The inclusion and subsequent maintenance of living flowers extends Chloë's ethic and approach to intimacy as a form of shared labor within the interpersonal relations that drive, and in fact co-constitute, the work in *The Book of Everyday Instruction*. The flowers were an expression of care, signalled by the repeated and durational attention that their upkeep required. My ongoing participation in this exhibition element reflects the way that Chloë's work inhabits and impacts her own lived experiences, and the experiences of her participants and audience. The work that makes up the expansive project that is *The Book of Everyday Instruction* exists most fundamentally outside the gallery; it takes place in daily life.

To locate the work within everyday life, attention must be paid. Chloë's multifaceted project hinges on the directive that unofficially introduces the show, an intervention she made on Knockdown Center's box office marquee stating: "I want us to look more closely." The exhibition's sprawling format encouraged visitors to look at all of their surroundings with the rigor and curiosity that one expects to bring to an arts space. *The Book of Everyday Instruction* not only inhabited Knockdown Center's two galleries, but also extended into the restrooms, the bar, the front patio, and the flagpole — common areas where Knockdown Center's various publics might encounter an intervention while attending events like concerts, conferences, festivals, and performances.

The work is driven by Chloë's poetic, rigorous, and generous investigations of various modes of social behavior wherein we might find unnoticed forms of intimacy. This is carried out in eight chapters, each of which is guided by a central question such as: How do we know when we're really together? How do we build a place through shared labor over time? What is the story told by the distance between two bodies in space? Inventive modes of documentation translate these interpersonal events though photographs, text, collage, rubbings, video, and installation. There are works in the galleries that visitors are invited to interact with, such as a stack of surveillance footage transparencies that can be viewed using a light box, a game for two people to measure the various registers of social distances using colored ribbons, jars of spices to smell, and a custom phone app that allows users to track and name colors in their immediate environment. Text interventions prompting the curious to stop and consider their relationship to their surroundings are found in unlikely spaces: on the mirrors and stalls in the restrooms, in unusual — nearly hidden — locations within the galleries, and outdoors on the front patio. There are also consumables: when using the restroom down the hall from the gallery, a visitor might discover toilet paper covered in text detailing intimate details about strangers; at the bar, one could enjoy a two-ingredient cocktail from a special *Book of Everyday Instruction* menu served with a custom cup and napkin embossed with text; viewers were offered a text-covered mint to savor as they entered or exited the show. The consumables suggest the ways in which art objects can be used as tools that serve a purpose in daily life, deemphasizing their material permanence in favor of the emotional reactions they elicit through direct interaction and use.

Finally, there were the flowers, punctuating the exhibition with small, colorful bursts of life and visibly marking the passing of time alongside artworks and interventions that more abstractly imply their own temporal depth, with each chapter marking complex layers of time spent. By the end of each week, the flowers would wilt or dry out. They were a reminder that as we go about our daily routines, all around us things are living and blooming and languishing and dying, adding a real weight to the questions that Chloë asks about how we approach life, and to the suggestion that we more actively care for one another.

After learning to look more closely, I think the question of how we might better attend to one another is at the heart of *The Book of Everyday Instruction*. The shift from looking to attending emphasizes a more present and engaged mode of observation, implies care as an imperative, and indicates the mutuality or reciprocality central to the production and reception of the project. In this sense, spending time is central to the production and reception of *The Book of Everyday Instruction*. Chloë proposes that the project consists of a series of individualized "performances without an audience," in its emphasis on private shared experiences, which necessarily unfold over time. Because the work is produced in relation to performance, the type of attention one brings to witnessing a performance is the type of attention that may best serve the project: durational and engaged. While the work contains a mixture of elements that range from archival to participatory, all aspects make space for the viewer to come closer, to register an emotion, and to share a private interaction.

The weekly flower ritual was my obligation to the exhibition, to Chloë, and to myself. It compelled me to slow down and to spend a quiet moment with *The Book of Everyday Instruction*. I was often overwhelmed with feeling during this time alone with my thoughts, the flowers, and everything that the exhibition contained. Working with Chloë on *The Book of Everyday Instruction* gave me simple tools for adjusting my approach to my practice, to the people around me, and to myself. Indeed, Chloë has offered all of us instructions that we can apply to our lives so that we can be better to one another. The world critically needs these tools.

There were always extra flowers. The leftovers tended to make their way onto the desks in Knockdown Center's office and into my home. And for eight weeks, these reminders of deeply emotional moments with *The Book of Everyday Instruction* punctuated my daily routine with cheerful color.

ALEXIS WILKINSON
Exhibition Curator
Knockdown Center
QUEENS, NY

CHAPTER ONE:

YOU+ME TOGETHER

you+me together

How do we know when we're really together?

The Book of Everyday Instruction, Chapter One: *you+me together* is a chronicle of time spent one-on-one. Cleveland residents were invited to spend an afternoon with me, engaging in an activity that the participant would normally conduct with a regular partner.

The 16 text and text-photo diptychs, 107 instant images, and ephemera that compose Chapter One represent time spent with 16 strangers. My participants and I shared activities ranging from dog walks, to beauty salon trips, to cemetery visits. The amount of time we spent together ranged from one to nine hours, and took place at all times of day.

Time spent together is imperfect. There is so much that we miss. Sometimes a great deal that we get wrong. This is one attempt at capture.

Chapter One originally premiered at SPACES (Cleveland, OH), and was produced entirely through the support of the Spaces World Artist Program (SWAP) residency.

WHEN:

March - May 2015

WHERE:

Cleveland, Ohio

FACING PAGE IMAGE: a screenshot of the original Craigslist
ad seeking project participants in Cleveland, 2015

ONE: Testaments

Between April 4th and 30th, 2015, I hung out with 16 strangers in and around Cleveland. Out of each of these experiences, I created a single image and associated text representing a moment of our shared time.

Each image is really two photographs placed together: one of the instant photos I took during my time with a participant, "framed" by my hand in my own immediate home environment — the cottage where I stayed in Tremont. Both the images and the text reflect my own input into the shared time — a placement of myself in the time that ultimately belonged to others.

These 16 photo-and-text diptychs make up the bulk of the exhibit, and constitute a finished work as a series. They are meant to be viewed together. Each diptych is named for the person with whom I shared the day.

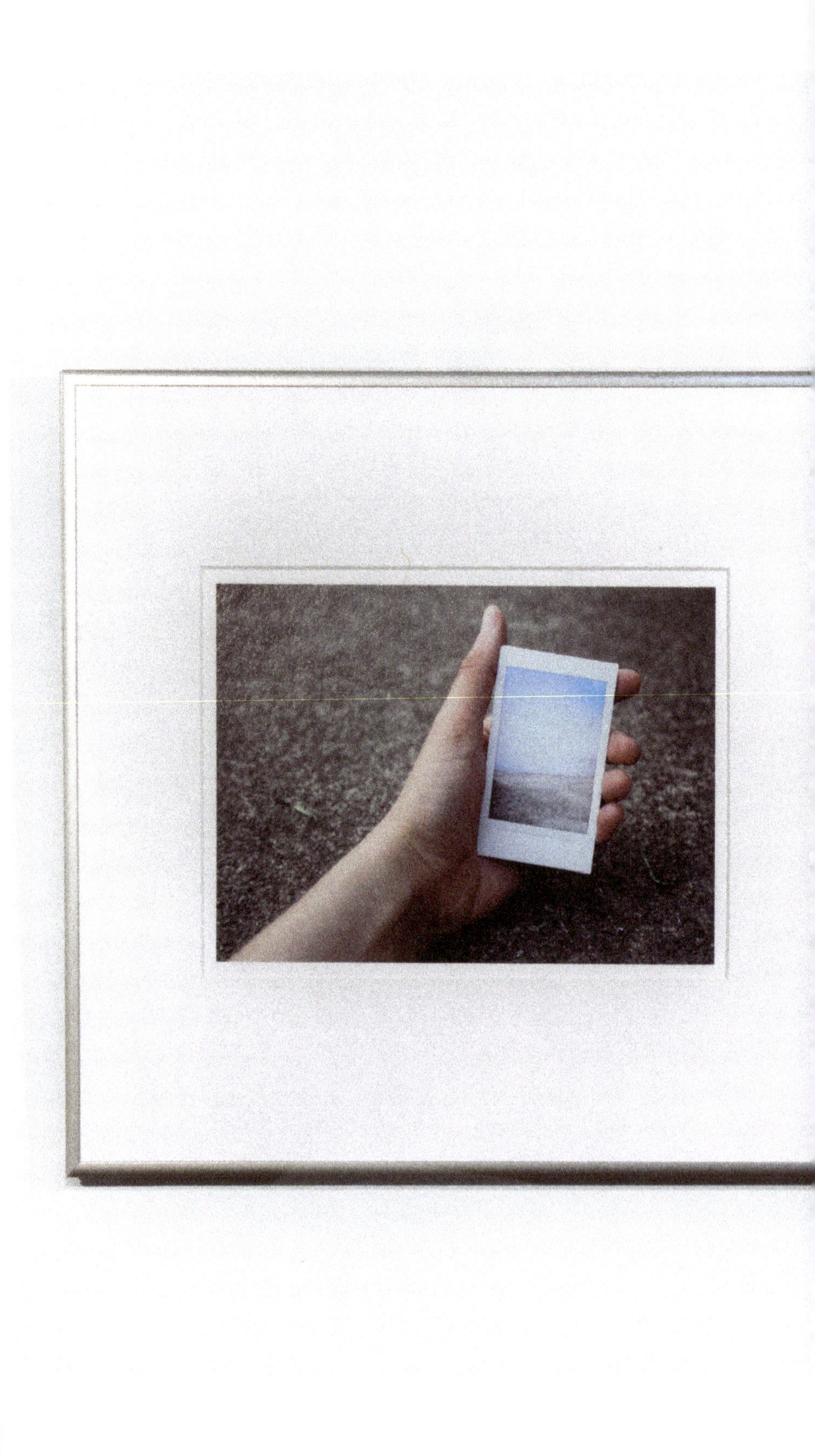

Sitting by the lake in the fog, two boys sprawled out at the end of the jetty, a young couple climbing on the rocks, while we talk about not much; 40 minutes, Cleveland, OH, April 2015.

Scenic overlook stop preceding discussion of his mother's final words; 1 minute of looking, Cleveland, OH, April 2015.

A detour off the highway, 8 minutes, and/or thank goodness we are both slender people who can slip through this fence; 3 minutes; Cleveland, OH, April 2015.

FROM TOP: Shane, Jeff

Two questionable Japanese meals eaten in a mall food court while talking about family dynamics and personal growth; 2 hours (more or less), Cleveland, OH, April 2015.

Stopping briefly during a tour of the Morgan Conservatory, bumping up against old wooden shelves (I bruised my knee); 2 minutes, Cleveland, OH, April 2015.

Two activities conducted simultaneously as a form of preparation, the inability to co-exist fully in both: a family dynamic; 14 minutes, Cleveland, OH, April 2015.

A car ride to the lake so that we can do some walking; 20 minutes or less; Cleveland, OH, April 2015.

Trotting through Lakewood to avoid waiting too long at the bus stop, turning every few minutes to see if the bus is catching up to us yet; 25 minutes, Cleveland, OH, April 2015

A muddy walk, just after almost slipping (and before almost slipping again), as we laugh; time unknown, Cleveland, OH, April 2015.

FROM TOP: Laila, Teresa, Mimi

Brief moments of heat between observation of historic graves, interaction with strangers, time spent in the car; 15 seconds (repeatedly), Cleveland, OH, April 2015.

Time spent together in the living room after dinner, answering questions and finishing a bottle of red wine; 52 minutes, Cleveland, OH, April 2015.

Sitting by the lake in the fog, two boys sprawled out at the end of the jetty, a young couple climbing on the rocks, while we talk about not much; 40 minutes, Cleveland, OH, April 2015.

FROM TOP: Tracy, Jack, Heather

One orange eaten together over the course of three minutes (me) and much longer (her), interrupted by a family visit; 20 minutes in total, Cleveland, OH, April 2015.

Stopping at the intersection as the sun continues to rise, 30 seconds; Cleveland, OH, April 2015.

Stepping out of the car to catch the picture of a place we didn't go, car's engine still running, cold outside, but sunny; 2 minutes, Cleveland, OH, April 2015.

FROM TOP: Josiane, Julie, Gwendolyn

A beer and a whiskey after an excruciating film, still sitting on hard seats, talking about love; 25 minutes, Cleveland, OH, April 2015.

Inking and pulling and printing and placing the papers on the floor, on repeat, best achieved with four hands and not two; 35 minutes, Cleveland, OH, April 2015.

TWO: Evidence

I have chosen to include the "evidence" items from the time
together to demonstrate alternate ways of marking time. The
full photo and text series stands on its own as one story.
The story of the film trash is equally important to me: it's
an archive that built itself over the work of my shared days
in Cleveland. The archive of accumulated materials means
something too — each item links me back to a specific moment
within a larger interaction. Evidence items are carefully
labeled and meant to be read.

ephemera bag: Mimi

ephemera bag: Laila

assorted ephemera bags

CHAPTER ONE: *you+me together* as installed at the Knockdown Center, 2018

THREE: Experience

A great deal of this project was shared in its most direct sense only between me, and the person with whom I was spending time. The other elements of the exhibit represent that time, but they do not entirely replicate or mimic it. As such, your experience in moving through the exhibit is as valuable as the research experiences I had in making it. I am hoping to give you ways of marking your own time here — perhaps a time you can share with someone else in your daily life.

Imagine the space like a dance. Partner up.

(Activity cards have been provided.)

activity cards as installed at the Knockdown Center, 2018

Formally, the only thing interesting about cruising for sex (in a perhaps by-gone sense) was its indetermining intervention (in the Cage sense) into the sorting of human interactions. By allowing one syntax (sex) to override other normative syntaxes (codes of hierarchies, transactional politeness, domesticated courtship, etc.) and thereby drive a given semantic field (types and classes of person), otherwise unthinkable interactions could come about. A banker in the bushes with a dock worker. A professor in a porno theater with a vagrant. These are the kind of interclass interactions Samuel Delany categorizes in his book *Times Square Red Times Square Blue* (1999) as "contact" sociality. This he opposes to "networking" sociality, those forms of interaction which would operate within and according to the rules of particular syntaxes of given social groupings.

As easy as it might be to position Chloë Bass' work in alignment with the task of imagining the kind of "contact" valorizing institutions Delany envisions at the end of his book, Bass' project lies elsewhere. She presents us instead with a much murkier situation in which "contact" and "networking" are all but indistinguishable. Crucially, sex is the only thing explicitly off-limits in the open call for participation in this first chapter of *The Book of Everyday Instruction*. For Bass, the problem of this confusion of ways of being together precedes sex. For Bass, as worked through in *The Bureau of Self-Recognition* (2011- 2013), the first question is the relation to the first other: one's self.

Let's turn our attention to the culmination of the *Bureau* for a moment. What became squirmingly apparent as the subject matter of the show and book were the complex narcissistic dynamics at play in social practice and recent participatory arts at large. Videos depicting individuals variously describing their fields of expertise, visitors gazing into a vanity mirror while performing one of Bass' self-recognition exercises, indeed the entire quasi-therapeutic conceit of the project, seemed to work as a kind of narcissism-provoking ruse not unlike so many instances of self-help or social media, but in this case, with no form of output but the cold light of the gallery. But beyond such an exterior oriented self-reflexivity, and leading us back to the current body of work, the *Bureau* also included the series of photos entitled "Practice of the Daily." Here, the question of narcissism appears in its illegibility to a viewer. That is, a series documenting everyday scenes and objects that contain some form of investment for their photographer, but for a viewer remain empty. Narcissism laid bare in its incommunicability, legible as such by their place in the overall discourse of the exhibition.

If the *Bureau* invited us to occupy the coolly reflexive position of the analyst, *you+me together* offers something significantly more complex – inviting even, let's say, counter-transference. The constellation of works that make up the show offer a constant push and pull of intimacy and distance. Lost in the digital visual plentitude of a languidly outstretched arm (here we require the distinction between an experience invoking primary as opposed to egotistical narcissism) we stutter upon the photo within the photo in the subject's hand (the gap of marking an unsharable personal investment now legible in the image itself). Lost in that recursive vertigo of the images within images (a quotation suggested by the artist: "Vertigo as a symptom of profound attraction. An excess of desire.") we stutter against each print's descriptive photo mate. And lost in the meta-poetics of the gap between image and description, we stutter onto the various quasi-sociological presentations of data punctuating the diptychs.

Though constructed from traces of Bass' casual encounters throughout Cleveland, the setup of the space, the primacy of the photo-diptychs, the sensual weight of the images' materiality, reveal that ultimately we, her viewers, are now the primary object, the ones being cruised. Roland Barthes states in *The Pleasure of the Text*:

> Does writing in pleasure guarantee – guarantee me, the writer – my reader's pleasure? Not at all. I must seek out the reader (must "cruise" him [sic]) without knowing where he [sic] is. A site of bliss is then created. It is not the reader's person that is necessary to me, it is this site: the possibility of a dialectics of desire, of an unpredictability of bliss: the bets are not placed, there can still be a game.

If the utopia of cruising was always already also the utopia of narcissism, personal or impersonal, Bass suggests something else altogether: a dynamics of relation, a dancing of position, an erotics of unending sequence.

written for the original *Chapter One* exhibit at SPACES in 2015

CHAPTER TWO:

THINGS

I'VE SEEN

PEOPLE

DO LATELY

Things I've seen people do lately

What is the pairing described by voyeurism?

Things I've seen people do lately focuses on what it means to be a pair when only one person (the watcher) knows the pairing exists. Described as "part observation-based text installation, part video peephole," the chapter demonstrates the poetics of how people come together accidentally.

Half of the information from this chapter was produced via direct observation of people and situations in Bed-Stuy, Brooklyn, where I live. The other half was produced via remote observation: watching publicly accessible surveillance livestreams online.

The materials produced for *Things I've seen people do lately* consist of four interconnected parts: a dual-channel video sculpture, featuring a short text piece and a collection of 61 surveillance screenshots which were also reproduced on transparencies, an associated text-based poster, 16 "blank" prints with imaginative text labels, and a participatory voyeurism exercise.

Chapter Two originally premiered at at the Salisbury University Art Galleries Downtown in Salisbury, Maryland.

June – August 2015

Bed-Stuy, Brooklyn;
other remote locations
via the internet

We know – or think we know – the discomfort of surveillance. At the security line at JFK, the agent sidles up to me: "Are you traveling alone?" "What?" I say. He looks at me again. I go through the scanner, accept a gentle patdown on my hair. The agent squirms through after me. I freeze. He looks at me hard: "No, I just thought you *was* someone." Afterward, I notice how much more interesting everyone is when I am by myself. Anyone can become someone for an instant.

I WANT YOU TO
LOOK MORE- CLOSELY .

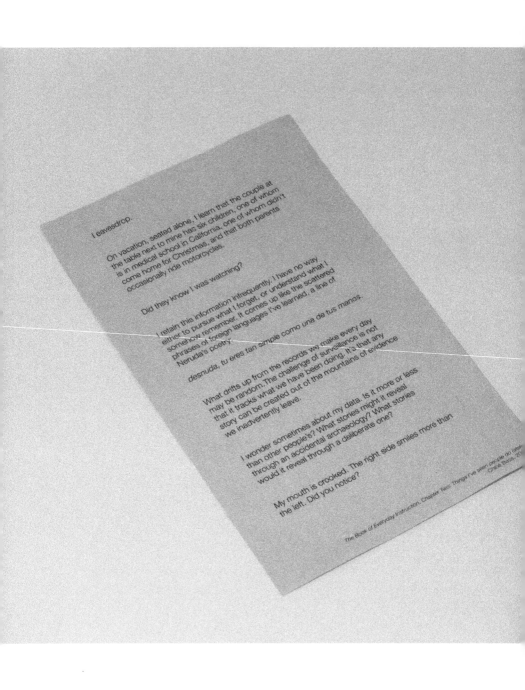

I eavesdrop.

On vacation, seated alone, I learn that the couple at the table next to mine has six children, one of whom is in medical school in California, one of whom didn't come home for Christmas, and that both parents occasionally ride motorcycles.

Did they know I was watching?

I retain this information infrequently. I have no way either to pursue what I forget, or understand what I somehow remember. It comes up like the scattered phrases of foreign languages I've learned, a line of Neruda's poetry:

desnuda, tu eres tan simple como una de tus manos,

What drifts up from the records we make every day may be random. The challenge of surveillance is not that it tracks what we have been doing. It's that any story can be created out of the mountains of evidence we inadvertently leave.

I wonder sometimes about my data. Is it more or less than other people's? What stories might it reveal through an accidental archaeology? What stories would it reveal through a deliberate one?

My mouth is crooked. The right side smiles more than the left. Did you notice?

The Book of Everyday Instruction, Chapter Two: Things I've seen people do lately
Chloë Bass, 2016

Things I've seen people do lately,
free open edition poster available for public distribution

I eavesdrop.

On vacation, seated alone, I learn that the couple at
the table next to mine has six children, one of whom
is in medical school in California, one of whom didn't
come home for Christmas, and that both parents
occasionally ride motorcycles.

Did they know I was watching?

I retain this information infrequently. I have no way
either to pursue what I forget, or understand what I
somehow remember. It comes up like the scattered
phrases of foreign languages I've learned, a line of
Neruda's poetry:

desnuda, tu eres tan simple como una de tus manos.

What drifts up from the records we make every day
may be random.The challenge of surveillance is not
that it tracks what we have been doing. It's that any
story can be created out of the mountains of evidence
we inadvertently leave.

I wonder sometimes about my data. Is it more or less
than other people's? What stories might it reveal
through an accidental archaeology? What stories
would it reveal through a deliberate one?

My mouth is crooked. The right side smiles more than
the left. Did you notice?

The Book of Everyday Instruction, Chapter Two: Things I've seen people do lately
Chloë Bass, 2015

People may be unaware of being photographed in a variety of situations, installation view, Upfor Gallery, 2016.

People may be unaware of being photographed in a variety of situations, transparency installation view, Knockdown Center, 2018.

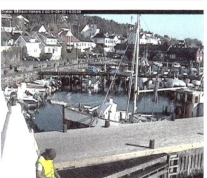

pp 44-51: screenshots from 61 different surveillance
livestreams, 2015.

Running up the stairs after a young Black boy, an older White woman cries out, "wait! You lost your toothbrush!"

Things I can deduce from riding the train this morning: a lot of people were running a race today.

Vintage midnight blue Chevy truck with the Arkansas plates, I like your style.

Older white man earnestly explaining to younger Asian woman: "We're not Patsies over here."

Grizzled, tough looking man sitting on the front steps of his stop, patiently making a beaded necklace for the kitten at his feet.

Someone outside calling for his father so plaintively, and so loudly, alternating between *dad*, *daddy*, *pop*, just before dawn on a Saturday morning.

FACING PAGE: *Things I've seen people do lately*, as installed at the Knockdown Center, 2018.

A tiny child watching me apply my mascara on the train. When I catch her staring, she grins at me broadly, then turns to her mother to explain that her art teacher taught her class to shade under the nose and eyes in their portraits *to make it more 3D*.

The guy biking down Lewis Avenue balancing a 6-foot folding table, smoking a cigarette, and talking on his phone, all while not wearing a helmet.

Two classes of preschoolers bopping in the dairy aisle to Pretty Young Thing over the in-store sound system during their Halloween trip to the local supermarket.

A woman doing Bible word searches (one verse per search).

She tells me she wants to travel. She tells me she's joining the Peace Corps. She tells me she's teaching herself Korean.

Facing the corner of the bridge walkway, looking pensive, leaning into the surrounding city, quietly urinating.

Sad looking people blasting the radio and eating peaches in the lake's 4 PM sun.

The elderly couple in front of me in line at the store, buying only half a gallon of Rocky Road and a liter of Sauvignon Blanc.

The wholesome looking people sitting next to me have switched from glasses of milk to pony bottles of Smirnoff.

Staring down at her lap, smiling.

CHAPTER THREE:

WE WALK

THE WORLD

TWO BY TWO

We walk the world two by two

How do we build a place through
shared labor over time?

We walk the world two by two is a series
of four permanently installed cast aluminum
historic plaques that document on going two
person exchanges along South Elm Street. The
project memorializes small moments of personal
history from the everyday lives of community
members. The goal is to make public otherwise
unseen and unremarkable events, highlighting
them as an essential element of how we develop
place over time.

For *We walk the world two by two*, I interviewed
subjects in pairs, allowing the relationship
between the subjects, rather than between
subject and interviewer, to guide the process
of forming and historicizing lived truths along
South Elm. Each plaque has a corresponding
edited audio interview, which is available
both to remote listeners online, and geotagged
to the plaque's location for passersby in
Greensboro.

Chapter Three premiered, and exists as a
permanent public installation, in Greensboro,
North Carolina. The project was commissioned
by Elsewhere as part of South Elm Projects,
and was produced with the support of ArtPlace
America.

WHEN:

July 2015 - September 2016

WHERE:

Greensboro, North Carolina

IN THIS STORE, MARY WELLS HAS
ENCOURAGED VISITORS TO TOUCH
OBJECTS FOR THE PAST 46 YEARS.
SHE RELATES TO FURNITURE AS
THOUGH IT WERE PEOPLE,
TELLING US ABOUT HISTORY
THROUGH THE FEEL OF WOOD
OR GLASS. THE STORE HAS
ALSO SERVED AS A SECOND HOME
FOR MARY'S TWO DAUGHTERS.

We walk the world two by two (Mary Wells), rubbing, 2016.

Mary Wells. 607 South Elm Street, Greensboro, North Carolina. I first started in business at this location and the building next door 46 years ago, and seven years ago downsized to just this building. I have been in the antique business that long. Really, I have a love affair with history and old buildings. It truly was a love affair with this part of town. I had no desire to be in any other part of Greensboro. Downtown should be the center of a city community-wise, historic-wise, business-wise. It doesn't always hold true all through the years because of the exodus of department stores from center city out to malls. I have just always wanted to be here.

I used to be in a store up the street to the right of the drugstore. I started there and was there for about two years. Then were able to purchase the building right next door at 603-605. It used to be a feed and seed store. There was a big potbellied stove in there. There was a huge safe because they did not use banks back then. They had to keep their own safe, hope they remembered the right combination every morning. You could see in the backroom where there was a huge hole in the roof where the hay truck would come and drop seed and hay down. Of course, the dust and everything that came with it would come flying all through the store.

Then, this building was a dry cleaning, Wade's Dry Cleaners. You can still see the rods in the next room where all the clothes hangers were pushed all down the line. In the back room there was nothing but plug-ins all along the walls for the washing machines and the dryers.

My daughters grew up down here. Lisa, who is nonverbal, has wandered off up and down the streets way back in the beginning. She's 43 now. She would go down an alley so fast, just exploring, and cross the streets and so forth. I would get phone calls. "Did you know that Lisa is up here at our store?" "No. I didn't know she was up there."

We were always open on Monday nights until 9 o'clock. Got a lot of people, of course, after work. Now we get people who come in on Saturdays and say, "Well, you're never open." We say, "We are always here from 10 to 5 Monday through Saturday, but we get tired and go home at 5 o'clock. You're able to walk downtown and go to eat, but we want to leave downtown and go home."

Truly, the love affair was with the buildings and, of course, the people. There are a lot of people who still run these stores who have been here, not quite as long as I have, but close. We have developed relationships and we care about each other. We watch out for each other. Most of the time I would go on deliveries so that I could see where it was going to be placed in somebody's home. It just thrilled me to be able to buy unusual pieces like back bars that would come out of drug stores, and pretty mirrors that came out of dime stores or fancy restuarants.

It's sad to me that we feel like, because we grew up with certain pieces of furniture and things that we had in our homes, that we never care to see them again. I think that's like punishing that piece of furniture because it happened to be in a home where the people were not happy. It all comes from people and what their lives, their roots, were. How they have evolved, how they have become happy or not become happy.

To me, I guess, I relate to a piece of furniture as if it were a person because it can speak to me and tell me its history by looking at the back of it, how it was made, how it was hand-planed, how the boards were hand-cut, not by machine. Now, at 73 or 74, whichever one I am, I am beginning to realize that I do have to start letting go of many things that I have collected. You'd be surprised some of the things that people collect. They collect razor blades. They collect the old hand razors. Oh, goodness. They collect Depression glass. They collect different kinds of potteries.

They collect old clothes. I'm dealing with that now because I'm discovering in my warehouse boxes of old clothes. These are 1800s dresses and clothes. They will have turned yellow because of the type of boxes that they were stored in. Do I try to wash them in the bathtub with light Clorox? Then, of course, they all have to be ironed to look pretty before they come in the shop. I'm beyond all that type of work.

The longer I stay in business, the more change I see, the less interest I see in what I want people to be interested in. I'll have parents come in and they'll say, "Don't touch this. Don't touch that." I have to speak up and say, "I understand where you're coming from, and I understand that, yes, things can be broken." In a museum, people are upset because they cannot touch. In my place of business, I want children to touch. I want them to know what wood feels like, real wood. I want them to know what a vase feels like.

Then I start giving lessons around the store. Cut glass, a little will say, "Why is that called cut glass?" I say, "Well, run your fingers down the side of it." He says, "Woo, it almost cut me." I said, "Mm-hmm. That's why it's called cut glass." Then we have pressed glass. Then we have colored glass. It just goes on and on.

Several weeks ago, I had a typewriter sitting on a table or a desk up there at the front door, an old black one. A little boy came in and said, "Mom, this has got to be one of the first computers." I went over and told him, yes, it was. I showed him throughout the store of how the computer did evolve from typewriters. It's much more fun than looking at something in the textbook.

I'm being made to realize that, of course, the world is not all about my furniture and wood, but in the world today we need each other. We need to understand what each other feels and thinks, how they operate, because we can learn from each other. It pleases me that young people want to learn from each other.

Stephanie Sherman:

My partner in telling this story is George Scheer. We've been friends since 2002 and collaborators since 2003. We've been through, I think, everything that a person can be through together. Love, near death, starting a business, managing people, and I think we want to continue collaborating as long as we live. We'll probably also be best friends as long as we live. Sometimes, those are the same things and sometimes those are not the same things.

George Scheer:

This is my partner and friend, collaborator, muse, Stephanie Sherman, whom I have been friends with since 2002, and collaborating with since 2003. I remember the first time I saw Steph and I remember the first time I met Steph. One was where I dropped a flyer in her lap and the other was when she passed through campus, which was shortly before I dropped the flyer and then we began working as writers together.

Do you remember the smell when we first came in? It's still there. Do you remember ... I have a few things. Do you remember flashlights on the second floor into the room full of toys before they were all brought downstairs? Do you remember the first time you came before we even started? When you and Lauren were first driving down to see? Do you remember a candelabra when sweeping for the ghost story and listening to Ulysses?

Stephanie Sherman:

Yeah, I remember there was a possum in the living room. Do you remember the day that Alex said he was going to go live upstairs for 24 hours? Before we found Elsewhere, we were struggling with all these questions that were about how you just endlessly critique something without making anything and how easy that is and how it would be so much richer and probably more interesting to actually figure out what it would be like to invent the alternatives. Our education was so theoretical, right?

We never did anything. We just asked questions and asked questions and took things apart and took things apart. At a certain point, you just realize that you've been like a meth addict and everything has been taken apart. Don't you feel like then, that Elsewhere was, "Wait. Here's a way that we could put things back together in a totally different way?"

George Scheer:

It was always within the process of storytelling -- there was an early sense of adventure defined around making the story, seeing the story in the space, and the environment and the things, that confirmed the story that we were making. Then the occasional terrors of whether or not you can turn around or change things or whether you actually have any control over what all is happening, right?

Then the insistence even then to be telling stories. Even in those moments where it's like, this is not the story I want to end up telling. Like really insistently going back into it. I think that that has shaped a certain kind of mechanics over time, that we've related always to the building.

Stephanie Sherman:

At least for me, a big part, and there's also different dynamics in my family than George's. I dreamt of the sort of generosity that your parents bestowed on your beliefs and also what you were doing. They also knew you were doing a service to a ... Like, at least in part, right? You were dealing with a family legacy and contending with it and that was obviously, we're supporting.

Where I feel like in some ways, that's obviously a little bit more complicated for my parents to be understanding the benefit of supporting that kind of thing, but those generosities, they're not his role. Not everybody has a giant warehouse building sitting around full of things and the time and safety net to spend five years sorting it out.

George Scheer:

I don't remember that you and I have ever really directly talked about it, but your joining my family's narrative, but I don't know at what point that we had always talked about it.

At what point it became visible that the kinds of relationships or the space, what have you. I don't know. That's one thing. Something about that was invisible to us even though we talked about, from the beginning, our role, right?

That was the whole thing, was how do you build ... Part of our thinking about organization-wise was always about, how do you build something sustainable within an environment that's going to inevitably change it and help secure some of the character of that place?

Stephanie Sherman:

The building contains yesterday's weather. The temperature inside is yesterday's weather. I just want to put it in there that I think ...

George Scheer:

It's true. Yeah. It is always yesterday's weather. It's only the last bit that will be yesterday's weather, but it always feels like you know it's going to be cold in there today because it's rainy and cold yesterday. Having you present in this way is really important for the history of the organization and of the building. Historicizing your name into it. It's like people sometimes will ask, "When is Steph coming back?" Right? It's like, Steph is gone. She's here, but there's not like a ... You know what I mean? Even though you totally would. But I also think that in terms of the building and how people are coming in and how it will live beyond us, which is I think what the next phase is.

Stephanie Sherman:

Elsewhere has always been about complexifying the idea about what a home is and for me, the idea that I'm coming back is part of that complexity, right? Always coming back. Like, when is the next time I'm going to come back?

George Scheer:

Right.

Stephanie Sherman:

I'm also a nomad. At this point in my life, I really don't feel like I have one home. Greensboro is as much a home as anywhere I can imagine living. It's the place I've lived longer consistently than anywhere else. The idea about having a home somewhere that's a shared home, that you can always return to is pretty exciting, I think, as a concept for what it means to live in a world in which many people are rerouted and leaving for reasons more important than my own. How we live as nomads in the world with shared homes is something that seems pretty, pretty crucial.

The town transforming around us is a moment where our challenges of equity and who is a player in the new evolved Greensboro is incredibly pressing and part of our responsibility. Our challenges are making sure that we pass off the concept in a way that what feels like thousands of people who love it for reasons beyond loving us, that that's actually the reason that keeps it forward. It should be some memorial to what we dreamt of. It should be something that constantly reflects the present as a function of the past and future that have always been folded into the ecosystem that we imagine being called Elsewhere.

Trust isn't built in a month or a year. It's actually like a really hard ... You can go in with an intention to trust, but that's really different than actually trusting. Most times, it's solidified when things go wrong. Everyone has an Elsewhere, right? Their attic, their basement, the couch that they won't throw away for whatever reason. Those are part of our psychology of things.

Maybe they are like symptoms of this bigger condition we have of relating to stuff, but those are also the surplus slippages that made us human in this system that controls us. It's one way that we actually control it or relate to it beyond what it prescribes for us to do. The only thing consistent is that there's a collection of things in a building that is called Elsewhere. That's the idea of being an organization, not a collective or something else, is that ideally, in an organization, that that entity can be passed along.

I'm looking forward to how it's going to grow and how we'll grow with it and how you and I will grow up together. I think it's going to be great. It's fun to stand at this point and be like, "Okay. Now, we got time to grow up." Even after all these things that we put together and all the fears and things that we've shared. It's fun to remember having stood outside and just be like yelling at the sky about what we hope to see and what we thought could be.

SINCE 2003, GEORGE SCHEER AND STEPHANIE SHERMAN HAVE BEEN USING THIS BUILDING, AND THE OBJECTS WITHIN, TO CREATE COLLABORATIVE SYSTEMS THROUGH (IN)VISIBLE WORK AND PLAY. THEY HAVE ALWAYS PIECED THE WORLD TOGETHER IN DIFFERENT WAYS. THIS BUILDING REMEMBERS EVERYTHING: STORIES, REASONS, AND YESTERDAY'S WEATHER.

We walk the world two by two (Stephanie and George), rubbing, 2016.

FOR TEN YEARS, FOUR TIMES A
DAY, JERRY LEIMENSTOLL AND HIS
FAMILY'S DOG, WATSON, TOOK
LONG WALKS THROUGH DOWNTOWN
GREENSBORO. AFTER WATSON
DIED, STRANGERS WOULD STOP
JERRY TO ASK WHERE THE DOG
WAS, SOMETIMES CRYING WHEN
THEY HEARD HE HAD PASSED.
THEIR WALKS WERE A PART OF
THIS NEIGHBORHOOD.

We walk the world two by two (Jerry), rubbing, 2016.

Jerry

My real name is Gerald Leimenstoll.

Ramsay

My name's Sarah Ramsay Leimenstoll, but I go by Ramsay, and I grew up here until I went to college.

Jo

And my name is Jo Ramsay Leimenstoll, and Jerry and I got married in 1985, and we decided to buy a downtown building.

We moved in, in August of '87, and we bought it like August of '85, or fall or '85, we got married in May of '85 and then bought it and then did our design work and then hired the contractor. And I think it took them about nine months.

Jerry

Yeah, I'd say nine months.

Jo

I thought it was really important to keep a storefront there. I mean I wanted it to be a part of the street.

Jerry

I can't find a particular single moment for Jo. Who she is is exemplified by this building, I think, and what it is downtown. It's there, under it's own terms, and its own terms are very, very wonderful and very gentle. And I think that would be my comment on that.

Jo

We wanted to be here and our expectation was that downtown would come back and that we wanted to be a part of that. But it certainly was slow in happening when we first lived here. It was just dead. But I remember George's grandmother, Sylvia, she was a fixture, when we would take the kids she'd often come out to see them in their stroller, and of course she never wanted to sell anything. The thing people associated with South Elm was kind of on Saturdays you could come down and go in the shops, but there wasn't a lot else happening. And then across from what is now Gate City Boulevard, Lee Street, on this corner was a-

Ramsay

Fish market.

Jo

A fish market. And it had a giant billboard that was a mermaid. That was sort of like a, I was trying to tell people where we lived or how to find us, I would say, "Well you know the corner of Lee and Elm, where the mermaid is?" And everybody knew the mermaid and so you turn left there. So when we first moved here, the day labor pick up point was right here on this corner, across the street from us, and on our side, so when it rained, they would come, some of them would huddle inside of our little recessed entry and stuff.

And as Ramsay said, we had a nice rapport with them. They knew we lived here. It took a long time to get them stop urinating behind our building. It was sort of like, "Don't you know we see you?" That's what people thought of with this part of town was you could come pick somebody up to come do work for a day. Or you were going to the fish market, or on Saturday's you could come down to sort of spend the morning looking for antiques. And now, and people thought we were crazy when we bought this building and moved it here, it was like, we couldn't get a bank to give us a mortgage, they were like, "Yeah, we understand you can make the payments, but if you decide you don't want to live there, there is no one else who would, you know." But it was pretty redlined, I would say.

But now, I mean say people think it's hip to live downtown. You know it wasn't like Jerry and I invented that, it just, it hadn't really happened much in Greensboro at that point. So we were ahead of the curve on that. But now, tons of people live downtown and I find that people aren't so suspect. But they're often surprised when they come in here and see the space.

What resonates for me, continually, is the whole streetscape of Elm in this section, because it's got so much charm and character from the period of the buildings and because people weren't investing in it for a long time, the storefronts stayed. It has a different sort of ambience to it and character to the street, that is so far from being generic. It's what to me, is downtown. And there aren't that many cities in North Carolina that still have several blocks of that. So I love that there's all this new energy and new things happening, I cringe every time I see someone make choices about how to alter their storefront or the façade in a way that to me is showing a lack of understanding of the charm it has.

Ramsay

I think it's really great that there's so much more happening in downtown now. It's especially nice because when I come home, if my friends and I want to go to things that are within walking distance, we can. And I've always felt that people should spend more time downtown. Like, growing up, even my brother and I when we were kids would like scoff about how terrible like urban sprawl and white flight are for cities, and we're like, "It's just terrible what's happening to the American metropolis" and things like that. We're very glad that we didn't live on the outskirts and have to drive 20 minutes to get anywhere.

But I think a lot of people who are coming downtown now maybe don't, and it's easy to see why, but like if you kind of think that it was really dead before, I mean there were always people making a go of it. Like they had their store, or like there was something that they were really dedicated to and that people would go to constantly, but it was just a smaller group of people. And like there definitely was a dip, like when I was a little kid, Woolworth's was still open as Woolworth's and we'd go there with our babysitters and it was, it closed and was kind of dormant for a while, before it was the Civil Rights Museum.

And so there definitely was like a dip, but there have been stores that have been there the whole time, some of them are still here or some of them have converted or merged or moved and it's not like everything that's good about downtown is new since new people started investing in it or something. And we're really glad that there is Downtown Greensboro, Incorporated and Action Greensboro and stuff, but there's always been things to do and it's always been worthwhile to spend time down here.

Jo

I mean I remember people would say, "Oh, I've never been downtown." And I would say, "How can you live in Greensboro and you've never been downtown?" It just flabbergasted me.

Jerry

I think the stories are about people and that's what sort of what Ramsay is alluding to as well. I mean, you mention names and you mention places and the people who are here now, some of them were here 28 years ago, some of them are gone. That's just the way history works, I think. People come, people go, and people live, people die, and whatever else. But some of the people, like Bill Brooks, I mean he's been here before we were here. And he's a crazy guy, but he's a genuinely decent person and he knows everybody by name. And he's part of this community. When there was Southside Hardware, where The Artistic is, Southside Hardware was an institution for generations down here. And Jack worked at Southside Hardware his whole life.

Jo

Talk about how people kept asking what happened to us, I mean because Jerry walked our dog.

Ramsay

Four-

Jo

Four times a day.

Ramsay

Four, 45 minute walks, every day.

Chloë Bass

Lucky dog.

Jo

Yeah.

Jerry

For 10 years. And he died when you were-

Ramsay

2010. Summer of 2010.

Jerry

When you were in the last year of college, I guess.

Ramsay

It was when I was in New York before senior year.

Jerry

Yeah. But there, years went by when people would ask me, they'd see me on the street and say, "Where's your dog?" This was three and four years after he had died.

Jo

Well, and all kinds of people. And some of them would just burst into tears when Jerry told them. I mean it was like, he was, Jerry and Watson walking the street, was part of the neighborhood, and it's touching to me, just all the times he's come home and said, well. One time somebody was driving by and pulled over and was like, "Wait, what happened to the dog?"

Jerry

In the last few months here, what's going on now right around here is intense. Very intense. And it's very positive. It's the most I've seen happen in such a short time ever, since we've been here.

Jo

Well, and it's the closest to us. I mean, really things have been happening further away, and now I mean it's, right here.

Yeah, it took a while for things to come south of the rail road tracks. I realize that I'm finally not scared when people are going to like be disappointed and leave downtown. Like whenever Grimsley had their prom at the Empire Room, and I was like, "Oh, people are going to be downtown, I hope that they think it's cool, that they don't have a negative experience and then decide to never come back again." And now, it's like, and it was like The Green Bean, and it was like, "Oh, people my age are coming downtown, are they going to stay?" And now it's like, not, I'm not worried about that.

You feel like it's turned a corner so they're not, you're not worried whether they'll like it or not.

Yeah. Which is just, I just kind of realized that, that I was always kind of like scared that people weren't never going to come back, after they were like, and I'd be like disappointed-

Dis your neighborhood.

Or something.

IN THE EARLY 1960s, THIS WAS
WALTER JAMISON'S STOPPING
PLACE WHEN WALKING DOWN
SOUTH ELM STREET. BEYOND THIS
POINT HE DID NOT GO.
HE REMEMBERS THE BLUE-JEANS
SMELL OF BLUMENTHAL'S,
THE GREASY BAGS OF CHIPS
FROM WOOLWORTH'S, AND THE
UNWRITTEN RULES OF BEING A
YOUNG BLACK BOY.

We walk the world two by two (Walter), rubbing, 2016.

Walter Jamison

My name is Walter Jamison. I was born and raised here in Greensboro back in 1958.

Liz Seymour

I'm Liz Seymour, and Walter is a really talented artist.

Walter Jamison

So you say.

Liz Seymour

Walter is a really talented artist. We met over that and kind of just started talking. We've talked about Walter growing up as a black man in the south, and me growing up in a privileged north, white, middle-class, college educated ... Even now our experience of walking down the street is different, and walking into a store is different.

Walter Jamison

Right. Right.

Liz Seymour

That's the sort of thing that you can read in a book, but having somebody be willing to share his experience with me has taught me a lot.

Walter Jamison

Yeah. I know on Elm Street in Greensboro there was Woolworths on one side and the movie theater, the Center Theater and I think it was Kress store-

Liz Seymour

I think that's on the same side as Woolworth's. Yeah.

Walter Jamison

I'm trying to remember these things, but there was stores on the left side and stores on the right side, which was Woolworths. During those days, when mom would come to us and say, "Hey, we're going to Woolworths," like that was an exciting time, you know, Woolworths, because black folks were allowed to shop downstairs. We could come upstairs and order food at the counter but we wasn't able to eat there. So we would order our food and go and eat it somewhere else.

Liz Seymour

Even after the sit-ins?

Walter Jamison

No, this was before the sit-ins. Before. Yeah. As soon as you opened the door you could smell the peanuts and popcorn and chips and cookies and everything. I think about it now, I can still smell it. It's, I don't know, a psychological thing, but if I close my eyes and I walk into Woolworths it's like the smell, the sounds and everything in there. It was the best of times, you know, and it was the worst of times. I didn't know much about racism back then, but I knew there was a difference. I knew there was something wrong.

Liz Seymour

I moved to Greensboro in 1979 and when I moved here downtown was just over. All the businesses had moved out. Most of the storefronts were empty. South Elm Street was here, but it was like a movie set with no movie.

I don't have any history with Greensboro when the last time downtown had stuff going on in it, but what was South Elm Street itself like when you were a boy? I know that there was ... There were sort of two Greensboros that were ... I've been told that the railroad bridge on East Market was kind of the entryway from black Greensboro to white Greensboro, but did you spend any time down in this part, South Elm Street?

Elm Street? Yeah. A lot. There was a thrift store and there was ... Blumenthals was a little further down and to the right.

Liz Seymour

Oh, I remember Blumenthals.

Walter Jamison

Yeah.

Liz Seymour

Do you remember ... Do you know the sign that they have that says like if you don't get a receipt you get a carton of cigarettes or something like that? That sign is in the Historical Museum now.

Walter Jamison

Really? Okay. Yeah. Another thing was like all the white folks would shop on one side and the black folks on the other side of the street. I know it's a psychological thing, you know. It was just a thing. Of course Woolworths was on the right. But when we got to come over to Woolworths it was great, or Blumenthals, because it seemed like everybody did their clothing shopping at Blumenthals.

Liz Seymour

You talk about the way that Woolworths smelled. I remember the way Blumenthals smelled.

Walter Jamison

Yeah, that jeans smell. Yeah.

Liz Seymour

Yeah.

Walter Jamison

Believe it or not, it came just right from up the road, Cone Mill, which is also closed down now. That was huge.

Liz Seymour

But when you were growing up was downtown ... Did it feel like it belonged to you as much as it belonged to everybody else, or was that kind of like going-

Walter Jamison

Absolutely not. No. We could go ... We was allowed to go certain areas, but if we'd go too far it was like, "What are you doing in here?"

Chloë Bass

What was the boundary that you remember?

Walter Jamison

As far as I can remember it was, like I said, as far as Woolworth and then back home. Well, actually Sears, because you could go to Sears and-

Liz Seymour

So not south at all? Because Woolworths is just barely on South Elm Street, so no further south? Well, Blumenthals.

Walter Jamison

Blumenthals, yeah. Remember that little red building in the center of the railroad track, or right next to the railroad track?

Liz Seymour

Yeah.

Walter Jamison

Yeah.

That saloon-

Yeah, somewhere along in there.

... Was where you couldn't go any further?

Yeah.

So you knew that Forbes was down there but you also knew you couldn't go?

Right.

So where would you go for a soda?

Woolworths. Yeah. Soda, popcorn and chips. It was great because you wouldn't ... Today you get like a bag of chips, you know, you might have this much air and this much in chips, where back then chips came in a paper sack. This may sound weird, but it was exciting to see a greasy sack. You walk in and you're eating greasy chips, but it was okay. This was a big bag of chips and it was filled up all the way to the top for maybe a quarter to 75 cents. It was wonderful.

I wonder if it had to do with stores like Fordham's were locally owned? Woolworths was a national chain. I wonder if people felt more comfortable. Even if Woolworths had that history, but I think part of the reasons that the sit-ins were there rather than at Fordham's was because they could have a national impact.

Walter Jamison

Right. Right.

Liz Seymour

But I wonder if your mother, for instance, felt more comfortable at a place like Woolworths than a place that was locally owned?

Walter Jamison

My mother was really passive. That's why I blame some of my passiveness, from her, because she always would say, "You obey the rules," so I can't be mean to the white folks, white persons, like my friends were. They were out there with like irate ... They was able to speak out, "I hate you," boxing back and forth. Whereas me, I was like my mom said this is bad. We was church going folks. Okay, let me be humble. God is listening.

I never went to jail for something I thought was right. I always went to jail for what I knew was wrong. That's a big difference right there. I never stood up for righteousness so to speak.

Liz Seymour

Well, you have, but you just haven't gone to jail for it.

Walter Jamison

Right. Exactly. But I have went to jail for things that I've done wrong and knew they were wrong.

Liz Seymour

Can I ask what you went to jail for in Greensboro?

Walter Jamison

There was a lot of fights, you know. Stealing.

Was this when you were in high school?

No. I'd say before high school, maybe early parts of junior high. I didn't stay much in jail, but maybe a day or a half a day. I'd cry my eyes out until mom come and get me, that type of thing. "I should leave you in there." No, no.

I'm kind of attracted to the idea of historical markers of essentially what wasn't there, right? That invisible line that was never drawn.

Yeah.

It was never ... It wasn't painted in the street, but that everybody knew was there, and that now young people won't know that that invisible line was there because it's never been memorialized.

Right. Right.

The majority of Americans were born after the Civil Rights Movement, so your experience is growing more and more unique. Places where there was a sit-in do get memorialized, but places where people were just leading their daily lives, following the rules that everybody acknowledged and nobody ... But were never written down anywhere, I think those need to be memorialized also.

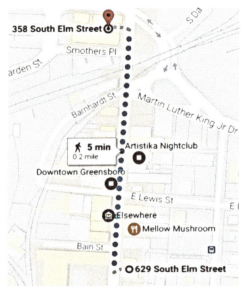

The route down South Elm Street. Google maps.

In 2015, I was invited to Greensboro, North Carolina, to do a project along a section of South Elm Street. This work was part of a series commissioned by Elsewhere, a museum and artist residency set inside a former thrift store, which is also on South Elm. Elsewhere's work focuses on the idea of collection. Most artists are invited to make new installations out of the things and materials already housed within the three-storey building. I was asked to do something different - to make a new work out of the stories and people already housed in the museum's neighbourhood. This made sense to me. Although I have a robust studio practice, I rarely work directly with materials, preferring instead to investigate interactions, engage in social research and utilise familiar, often pre-fabricated structures in poetic ways.

I wound up working with approximately a five-minute walk's worth of South Elm, from the railroad tracks on one end to almost the corner of Gate City Boulevard. But five minutes can mean many things - the shift from a safe place to danger, or the chance to run into a friend. As a New Yorker, I'm trained not to notice. I walk faster than North Carolina's more neighbourly pace. Five minutes in Greensboro can easily be spent between the one step and the next, saying "hey" to the people you encounter.

Jerry Leimenstoll with his plaque, permanently installed on the outside of his home on Greensboro's South Elm Street.

My project *We walk the world two by two* is a series of four cast aluminium historic plaques that document ongoing two-person exchanges along South Elm Street. The project memorialises small moments of personal history from the everyday lives of community members. The goal is to make public otherwise unseen and unremarkable events, highlighting them as an essential element of how we develop place over time.

Greensboro is a particularly interesting place in which to engage with ideas of who makes history. Somewhat further down the road from where I worked, South Elm Street is home to the Civil Rights Museum, set inside the Woolworth's store that housed one of the first integration sit-ins in 1960. The city is rich with history and its documentation, from the transformation of the store to a museum to plaques commemorating the inventor of Vicks VapoRub or a bust of Dr Martin Luther King, Jr. marking not a site where he visited, but where he didn't. Passive aggressively, this bust's plaque suggests that if he had made it to Greensboro rather than heading to Memphis perhaps he would not have been shot and killed.

But there's missing history too. Greensboro is an ideal place in which to examine systems of power and their impact on the creation and presentation of history. The city went through a long and detailed Truth and Reconciliation process following an outcry over the public representation of the 1979 Greensboro Massacre.[1] During a peaceful march against the Ku Klux Klan, five protestors were shot and killed by Klan members. When historical signage was put up to commemorate the event, the word "massacre" was considered too strong for public presentation, and ultimately eliminated: a quite literal whitewashing of the tragedy. Who gets to write history, and how that history can be either manipulated or erased, is an essential question anywhere, but one that seems publicly foundational here.

From left: the artist, Chloë Bass, Jo Leimenstoll, Jerry Leimenstoll.

'We walk the world two by two' is the third chapter of my ongoing work, The Book of Everyday Instruction, which explores one-on-one social interaction. Each chapter of the project focuses on its own idea of pairing, and its own central inquiry question. Chapter three's central question is, 'how do we build the story of a place through shared labour over time?'

For this project, I interviewed subjects in pairs, allowing the relationship between the subjects, rather than between subject and interviewer, to guide the process of forming and historicising lived truths along South Elm. There's a way that two people, especially two people who know each other well, can fact check each other simply through their use of tone and gesture, not to mention their desire to restate what each remembers as 'the facts.'

With my work, I wanted to emphasize and make public the ways in which daily, unsung labour over time — as much as, or possibly more than, important, change-making moments — turn a place into what it is. The variety of interviews I conducted helped my definitions of labour to widen: from artistic collaborations (George Scheer and Stephanie Sherman), to the work of making a family (Jerry and Jo Leimenstoll), to the maintenance of a business (Mary Wells), to the emotional labour of sharing space as a city-dweller.

Interviewee Walter Jamison, for example, told me about the unwritten rules of being a young black boy in the South — where he could or could not walk, where his mother was allowed to shop or not shop. There was no moment or story of conflict that he could particularly recall yet these boundaries were real for him and affect him even as an adult. Walter's interview partner, Liz Seymour, clarified his stories by sharing the ways in which she (a white woman) and Walter (a black man) will never have the same experiences walking down the street even now.

Walter Jamison and Liz Seymour holding Walter's plaque inside Elsewhere, pre-installation.

While working on the project I classified my own responses to my subjects and their places as a kind of falling in love. Every time I do a project that requires social participation I find myself falling into a wonderful listening place where everyone can be someone. I was in love with each of my interviewees, at least temporarily, and I held them with care in this way. I too was held with care in turn. I joined Walter and Liz as the third (honorary) member of the Greensboro Philosophers' Club. I got to ask people about things that felt like secrets and I got to treat these secrets with honour and care. I am not by nature a joiner. I am an only child. I celebrate the particular prickly state of attention that is produced by being alone in a public space. But as a person who thrives on finding poetry in the familiar there is perhaps nothing more intimately special than being entrusted with someone else's secrets. The best way to collect the material I love is through simple acts of being together.

In the throes of this work, my love began to extend further than my immediate subjects and collaborators. I started to look at everyone, at least for a while, as someone with a fascinating story. In my regular life as a jaded New Yorker it's hard not to view everyone and everything with a sense of scepticism and questioning. I often feel that this is the lens through which I am being regarded as well. But in the midst of a project about history something else happens. Everything comes to seem like a fascinating and essential part of how a place is made.

SINCE 2003, GEORGE SCHEER AND STEPHANIE SHERMAN HAVE BEEN USING THIS BUILDING, AND THE OBJECTS WITHIN, TO CREATE COLLABORATIVE SYSTEMS THROUGH (IN)VISIBLE WORK AND PLAY. THEY HAVE ALWAYS PIECED THE WORLD TOGETHER IN DIFFERENT WAYS. THIS BUILDING REMEMBERS EVERYTHING: STORIES, REASONS, AND YESTERDAY'S WEATHER.

George Scheer holding his and Stephanie Sherman's plaque inside Elsewhere, pre-installation.

At the end of each of my interviews I asked my pairs of participants to tell me what it would mean for them to have a plaque expressing their story embedded into their chosen building. I was delighted that the answers never included a banal expression of gratitude. Instead most participants focused on the idea of permanence. What does it mean to be on the map in this way? How does it feel to visit a record of one's own, now somewhat historicized, daily life? What does it mean if the record lasts longer than you do? Aluminium plaques are guaranteed to survive at least 50 years and Mary, my oldest interview participant, is either 73 or 74 (on the record, she couldn't remember). How will her plaque carry her daily life and work forward into the future?

Mary Wells with her plaque, permanently installed on the outside of her store on Greensboro's South Elm Street.

It's only a year and a half later. Mary Wells shut down her store this week although her plaque remains. I'm not in love anymore. There are lots of ways to measure time. To call it a five-minute walk misses the point entirely. But isn't labour always something hard-earned that other people can consume in an instant?

IN THIS STORE, MARY WELLS HAS ENCOURAGED VISITORS TO TOUCH OBJECTS FOR THE PAST 46 YEARS. SHE RELATES TO FURNITURE AS THOUGH IT WERE PEOPLE, TELLING US ABOUT HISTORY THROUGH THE FEEL OF WOOD OR GLASS. THE STORE HAS ALSO SERVED AS A SECOND HOME FOR MARY'S TWO DAUGHTERS.

A close-up of Mary Wells' plaque, permanently installed on the outside of her store.

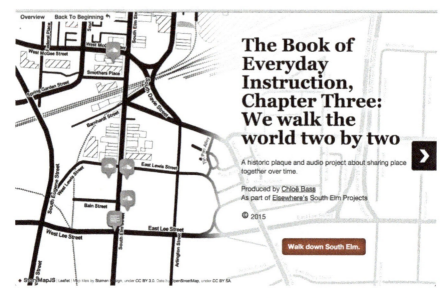

A screenshot of the We walk the world two by two interactive story map, produced using tools by Knight Lab.

NOTES:

1 Modelled after the Truth and Reconciliation process used in South Africa, the Greensboro Truth and Reconciliation process began in 1999, 20 years after the 1979 incident. For further information on the commission, including a detailed timeline of their work, visit http://www.greensborotrc.org/

2 This text was originally published in Living Maps Review No. 3, in the "Lines of Desire" section co-edited by Blake Morris and Clare Qualmann, in August 2017.

CHAPTER FOUR:

IT'S AMAZING

WE DON'T HAVE

MORE FIGHTS

It's amazing we don't have more fights

What is the story told by the distance between two bodies in space?

It's amazing we don't have more fights is focused on the accidental and incidental choreographies created by engaging with other bodies in space. This chapter uses the sociological field of proxemics to investigate forms of storytelling. The chapter's title paraphrases a quote from my mother about successful social behavior on New York's subways and buses.

Chapter Four consists of two short publications: *A Glossary of Proximity Verbs (Appendix A: Personal)*, and *A Field Guide to Museum Intimacy (Appendix B: Pedagogical)*, as well as a workshop performance, a series of short films, and a text installation in a shared, multi-stall unisex bathroom.

Chapter Four originally premiered at the Museum of Modern Art (*Field Guide*) and Lower Manhattan Cultural Council (*A Glossary* and the bathroom installation) as part of the 2015 - 2016 Workspace residency program.

February - May 2016

New York, NY

A FIELD GUIDE TO SPATIAL INTIMACY

The Book of Everyday Instruction, Chapter Four:
It's amazing we don't have more fights

(Appendix B1: Pedagogical)

PROLOGUE

I was talking to my mother about a recent experience on the subway. I had arrived at her apartment flustered, sweaty, late -- already exhausted and overwhelmed even without having faced the frustration of family. I don't remember what the offense was. Pushy people? Someone not using headphones? Whatever the cause, there was definitely a disagreement between two riders. This small tiff escalated until everyone in our car was involved, whether we wanted to be or not. I was furious, but hearing the story, my mother took the opposite approach. She believed that in fact, New Yorkers are mostly worthy of praise. "Really," she said, "when you consider that the subway is the space where our bodies are closest to people who are different from us, it's amazing we don't have more fights."

The Book of Everyday Instruction is an eight chapter project about one-on-one social interaction. Each chapter focuses on a different central inquiry question. Chapter Four, *It's amazing we don't have more fights*, investigates how we tell stories through pair-based physical interactions in space. Where are the guidebooks to teach us how to move in contemporary society? What are the lessons we might need? I am considering partnership from this perspective.

This booklet contains:

1. Exercises For Your Completion
2. Images For Your Enjoyment
3. Background Information For Your Understanding
4. Creative Writing for Your Stimulation

Each booklet comes with one (1) set of measuring ribbons, to be used in tandem with exercise #2.

EXERCISE #1: MOVING

Find someone in the room to:
a) follow;
b) avoid.

Then do it.

Find someone in the room who:
a) attracts you;
b) repels you.

Then do it.

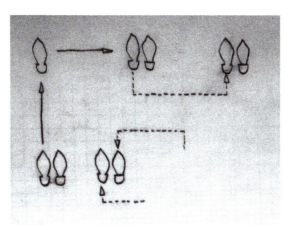

Figure 1. An incomplete diagram of feet in motion.

Proxemics is the study of human spatial requirements and the effects that population density has on behavior, communication, and social interaction. Proxemics is among several subcategories in the study of nonverbal communication. *(Wikipedia, 4/17/2016)*

This chart, developed by researcher Edward T. Hall in 1966, depicts his scientifically determined ideal distances between people sharing intimate space, personal space, social space, and public space.

Of course, these distances vary by culture (both ethnic, and locational). *The distance between us in line is far less than I'd like it to be if, for example, you were visiting my home or studio. Likewise, I imagine we'd feel differently about what was spatially appropriate if one of us were, say, Japanese. Or Kenyan. Imagine the posibilities.*

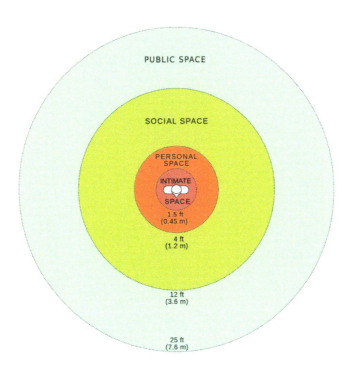

PUBLIC SPACE

SOCIAL SPACE

PERSONAL
SPACE

INTIMATE
SPACE

1.5 ft
(0.45 m)

4 ft
(1.2 m)

12 ft
(3.6 m)

25 ft
(7.6 m)

*I think our strong, almost instinctive feelings about
public spaces are formed by how close we are to
other people when we to experience them. There's a
built-in excitement to walking in a public square. It's
not the weather. It's the nearness of other bodies.*

EXERCISE #2: MEASURING

You have been given four ribbons. Each is cut to a different length. First choose a point of reference in the room. Using these measuring guides, position yourself each of the four distances away from that point. Note any changes to your relationship with the room.

Second, choose a partner from the workshop. Position yourself each of the four distances away from your partner. Note any changes to your relationship with your partner, or with the room.

You can start your measurements from smallest distance to greatest, or from greatest to smallest. For best results, try going once from smallest to greatest, and then in reverse.

An incomplete list of proximity verbs: chase, follow, lead, settle, approach, sidle, retreat, embrace, accompany, block, join, shake, tango, touch, unite, deny, shadow, engage, cleave, devour, divorce, merge, spoon, track, crave, protect, dismiss.

EXERCISE #3: STORYTELLING

There are so many verbs that we use to discuss relationships between bodies in space. (I call these "proximity verbs.")

Pick a verb, either from the list below or otherwise.
Keeping in mind the physical interactions that you've just shared in the gallery, imagine yourself in space with that verb.

What memories come up?
What relationships do you want to explore?
How does the story change as distance changes?

Using your piece of chalk, write a short story along the floor.
Maybe 1 - 4 sentences long.
Use the verb you selected as the title for that story.

(example)
PLAY

What if there was a way to play Memory that instead of matching like-images, you could first look at your partner's eyes, and then track their gaze to what was being observed? And if you guessed right, that would be a pair? The winner would be, I suppose, the person who best understands the link between the outward-facing expression of the body, and desire.

EPILOGUE

WHAT IS THE LARGEST DISTANCE?

Is it the distance before we come together, or the distance after we separate? When do we require more space? When we know there's a step back to be taken, or when we don't know that there's a term binding us at all?

PROLOGUE

I was talking to my mother about a recent experience on the F train. I had arrived at her apartment flustered, sweaty, late — already exhausted and overwhelmed even without having faced the frustration of family. I don't remember even what the offense was. Pushy people? Someone not using headphones? Whatever the cause, there was definitely a disagreement between two riders. This small tiff escalated until everyone in our car was involved, whether we wanted to be or not. I was furious, but hearing the story, my mother took the opposite approach. She believed that in fact, New Yorkers are mostly worthy of praise. "Really," she said, "when you consider that the subway is the space where our bodies are closest to people who are different from us, it's amazing we don't have more fights."

The Book of Everyday Instruction is an eight chapter project about one-on-one social interaction. Each chapter focuses on a different central inquiry question. Chapter Four: *It's amazing we don't have more fights,* investigates how we tell stories through pair-based physical interactions in space. What are the guidebooks to teach us how to move in contemporary society? What are the lessons we might need? I am considering partnership from this perspective.

This booklet contains:

1. Exercises For Your Completion
2. Images For Your Enjoyment
3. Background Information For Your Understanding
4. Creative Writing for Your Stimulation

Each booklet comes with one (1) set of measuring ribbons, to be used in tandem with exercise #2.

EXERCISE #1: MOVING

Find someone in the room to:
a) follow;
b) avoid.

Then do it.

Find someone in the room who:
a) attracts you;
b) repels you.

Then do it.

> Note how your feelings change as you follow and avoid. Note how your body changes as you follow and avoid. Note who is following and avoiding you. Does this change your feelings about that person?

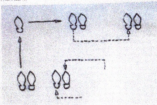

Figure 1 An icomplete diagram of feet in motion.

WHAT IS THE LARGEST DISTANCE? Is it the distance before we come together, or the distance after we separate? When do we require more space? When we know there's a step back to be taken, or when we don't know that there's a term binding us at all?

Documentation images from *A Field Guide to Spatial Intimacy*
at the Museum of Modern Art, NY 2016.

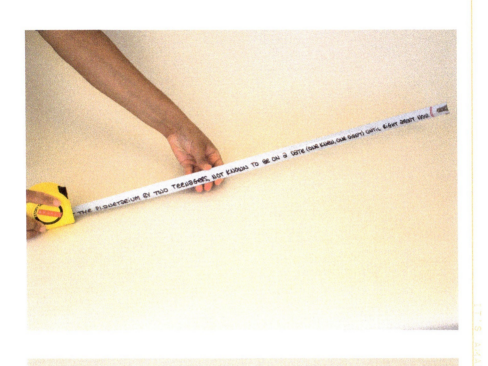

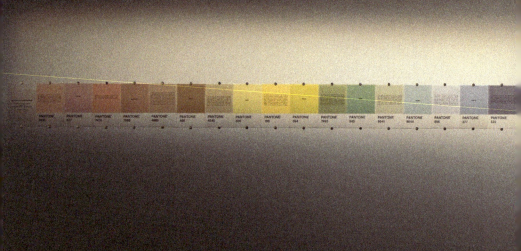

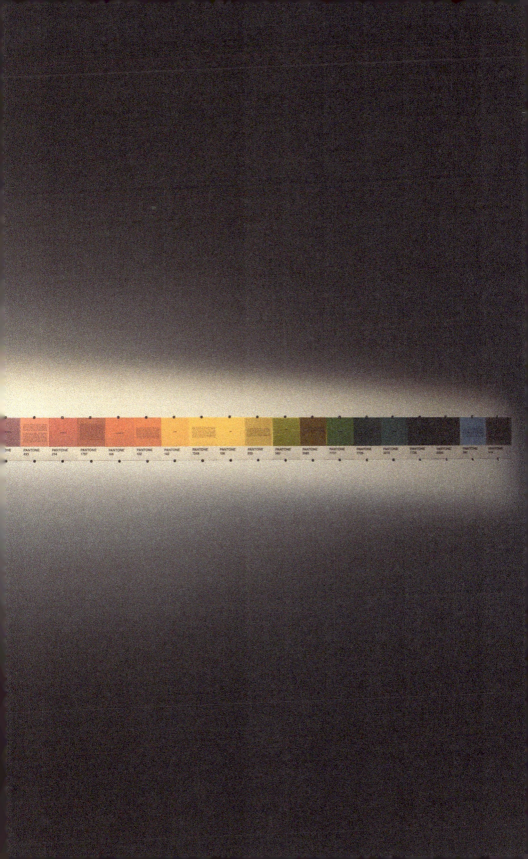

PREVIOUS SPREAD: *A Glossary of Proximity Verbs*
as installed at The Kitchen, 2018.

A GLOSSARY OF PROXIMITY VERBS

The Book of Everyday Instruction
Chapter Four:
It's amazing we don't have more fights

(Appendix A: Personal)

I am writing a glossary of proximity verbs, and dedicating it to you. Perhaps this is what you meant when you said I'm less careful than you are. It's true; I have less at risk. By which I mean: all of my mistakes are my own, and yours belong to other people, too.

Any experience can become a kind of definition.

FOLLOW

A few weeks ago you gave me a granola bar, which I found smushed at the bottom of my bag today and ate. Salt. Peanuts. Coconut. Every calorie warming me up against the chill of the day, the boredom of sitting still. You are fat, and pushy with food. You told me how you used to chase your children around with a spoon: *taste this. It's good.* I might have imagined the spoon. This morning you brought me eggs and toast, tiny tomatoes, soft little lettuces. I ate them too late, after we fucked, instead of right when I woke up, the way you had imagined. You have a problem with food; too much has challenged your body. I have a problem with you; the symptoms are somewhat the same. You urge me to see the doctor, get my bloodwork done. *I know it will be outstanding,* you tell me, but this is after we have agreed outstanding is a grade that doesn't really exist.

SETTLE

Eventually you can settle into anything, even sound. Beds, soft and warm. Patterns, if there's time to develop them. Anxieties, if they're constant.

APPROACH

I think what we'll need is music, or something more beautiful than music, to tease us out of the state we're in. The sound of your voice undoes me. I pause the video to hear the creak of your foot on the stair, the cough that always warns of your approach. I keep my hand on the doorknob to delay any opening, knowing that as soon as you step in, time will have moved from urgent waiting to the sick, nervous wane that comes after.

SIDLE

I dream of the day when I can call you beloved. This is a mistake. It is the kind of mistake that does nothing, but means a lot. I walk down the street with the hope of this mistake under my heels. It waits for me at the corner, sidles up to me in the supermarket line. The unreachable future. The unbalanced weight of hope.

DENY

In weepy, gentle conversation with my father about the desire for someone to share my home, he says, *yes, you're good in partnership*, which I don't deny. A few months later, I say to a girlfriend during an animated lunch, *maybe I should just be single*, and she brightly agrees, *for career reasons*. Neither of these things are more or less true. Neither comes closer to an explanation, either.

TRACK

We sit in the park. It is either the first day of spring, or an exciting phantom. *I've been looking at asses all day*, you say. *It's because I'm with you.* I track your eyes: dogs, babies, women. *Look*, you say, *there's a model*. *She looks regular*, I say, although she has a crown of hair and a ridiculous hat besides. My throat is sore and tight, the light a Los Angeles lemon haze. We are runaways in our shared joy.

PRICK

There were so many things I wanted to say but didn't. There was no space. We were manipulating something slippery like noodles. Or tendons. What would it be to cook our own meat, turn our bodies into something more easily digestible? When I don't hear from you it pricks me. Just a tiny bit. Like a pin slipping under a fingernail.

SHAKE

The feeling of being something precious, but expendable. If something has to go, it will be you. Last in, first out. Or else the more sinister hint that happiness is optional, while all else acquires unshakable meaning, a deep and precious weight, over time. Make a promise to yourself that you will be easy to shake. Mean it. This is the safest commitment short of letting go.

DEPART

You are gone for 29 days. The day before you left, I told you not to die during your trip. I said I would be angry if you did. You said you loved me, kissed me, kissed me again, said you loved me again, and departed down the steps to the B train. You looked beautiful and lost in the sun.

CRAVE

I had a strategy for your absence. I found a video of you clocking in at 1:14:49. I thought I would watch it for three minutes a day until you got back. It took me two days to realize that 1:14:49 is not 115 minutes, but rather 75. The result: 10 days at the end without a new trace of your voice. I'm not surprised that even with planning, I'm left with a great deal to crave. There is no planning against feelings, but pretending there might be makes the days go faster.

ENTANGLE

The first time I saw you, I was sick in bed with cramps, or maybe feverish. You had been dining in the lower apartment, and met my then-lover on the front steps. The two of you exchanged the greetings of dear friends; we were all so entangled already.

The child at the top of the stairs watching the party below believes she can't be seen. It's a special space of invisibility, like cats have. But a moment later your round face and his dark head turned upwards, towards my window, and I startled back, maybe yelped. Hot faced. Unwilling to come down. I didn't even wave.

PROTECT

You ask me if I have any archives. You mean the accidental ones, the collections we don't know we're making, or perhaps the purchase of other people's collections. I think of the suitcases of photos in Istanbul that served as slippery beds for sleepy cats hungry for sun. Where the light would fade the image, perhaps the fur protects. I never wanted one photo, I wanted all of them, and the suitcase, and the cat, and the sun to come with it, too. I tell you I don't have any archives, not even the accidental ones, and I think this has something to do with my thoughts about boundaries.

SACRIFICE

You sacrificed your socks the day you fixed the leak under my kitchen sink. I washed them and I wear them now. It is not until the second time I put them on that I notice your embroidered initial resting over the big toe on each of my feet. Seeing this, all the ideas that I've constructed around your life start to crumble. Such a tiny thing to teach me I know nothing.

LOSE

You're not very good at telling me what you want, you say, and I say *if I ask for one thing, I might ask for everything, and we both know that won't work.* I think: how can you have lived this long without realizing that the second desire is uttered, the utterer runs the risk of losing everything. That naming is in fact a form of theft. For the mother, birth is not a celebration, but the beginning of a lifetime of loss.

LIFT

I am running down the stairs to catch the G train and I feel my knee let go, just like that, and then I'm on the ground of the platform with a scraped chin and a bitten tongue. I call you and say *I hurt myself* and you come right away and lift me up. Or maybe I dreamed that.

TAKE

The only photo I've ever taken of you is horrible, and makes you look like a stunned mountain in a pink shirt. None of this was my intention but every time I look at it, it seems correct.

DISCOVER

You tell me that while you've been away, you've discovered a deeper love for me, and a deeper love for your daughter. You say you don't want to read too much into this. I don't need to tell you that I already have; you know I know what year she was born. I know you know I was born the same year. We make nothing out of this coincidence except for the occasional consideration and immediate dismissal of our relationship as cliché.

BATTER

I am always looking for a way out, except when there's no way in, and then I batter myself until I'm ragged.

SLIDE

A funny thing. Every time, with love, all the lessons I thought I had learned that I find myself unlearning. Such as: it doesn't have to hurt so much (but then, the heart says, *why not?*). Slide back to the beginning again: Chutes and Ladders, the craving to just make the game go longer. When you say *thinking of you*, do you mean once, or forever? How does it feel? Does it hurt?

I dream of the day when I can call you beloved. This is a mistake. It is the kind of mistake that does nothing, but means a lot. I walk down the street with the hope of this mistake under my heels. It waits for me at the corner, sidles up to me in the supermarket line. The unreachable future. The unbalanced weight of hope.

PANTONE®
4545

SIDLE

PANTONE®
466

A Glossary of Proximity Verbs (Sidle),
detail view.

Everything in this room has been left here so that you can perform one of the following functions:

1. Resting;
2. Texting;
3. Hiding;

Or you may choose to engage in a brief conversation with a partner.

Thank you for your participation.

You're about to make a choice.
Closest to the door, or furthest from it?

Statistically, I can tell you what you might do, but not
what it means about you.

If presented with three empty stalls, men:
Go left 26% of the time.
Go straight ahead 40% of the time.
Go to the right 32% of the time.

Presented with that same trio, women:
Go left 34% of the time.
Go straight ahead 29% of the time.
Go to the right 37% of the time.

But when the left stall is occupied, men:
Now head to the far right 73% of the time.

Women, under the same circumstance:
Move to the far right 65% of the time.

Given a line of identical options, people "reliably prefer
the middle one."

But of course I don't know what kind of person you
are. Only you know that.

And you don't know what kind of people they are.
Only they know that.

*I put these words in the bathroom because the bathroom is a place
where people read*, as installed at the Knockdown Center, 2018.

In the bathroom, I tell Tamar that I have boundary issues. I mean this in the context of saying no. Although what is a boundary if not a certain type of refusal. This is where I end, in the context of you asking for things. This is where you end, too. An inquiry with unmet desire turns a question into a statement, and the questioner into a kind of thud. If we both agree that it's an ending, maybe it won't feel so bad. Then we can walk away.

There's so much we learn as we share a private space. At what point does overhearing become a form of engagement? *I've finished people's songs in the bathroom — where someone is in there, and I don't think they realize someone else is in there, and they start to sing a pop song, and I finish it. Not the entire song, but the chorus.*

In the bathroom, Trokon tells me that this is the first time he's been in this unisex space with a woman and felt comfortable. "I guess that means we're friends now," I suggest, and he agrees. The moment quickly passes, but I don't forget it.

At one point in high school, my friend and I were talking about how we wanted to get some Adderall after school. We were in a rebellious time in our lives. We walked out of the stall, and my teacher was right there. She wound up calling my parents to the school, and having a whole discussion with my parents. It ended up blowing over. It wasn't a big deal, but it was a scary moment. It was probably the most scared I've ever been in my entire life. Normally fear is not my number one emotion.

As I consider what's appropriate, I realize a funny thing happens to people when they're in a shared space of addressing basic needs. The bathroom is the primary space where you can't avoid that you're a body, the intense denial of "I thought I was just a brain," "I thought I could just be language." Sacha tells me about a job interview that she conducted partially in the bathroom, due to unavoidable needs on the part of both the interviewer and the Interviewee.

Companionable peeing erases boundaries, in this case for the worse (the candidate didn't get the job). But mostly the result is equalizing: *I've made so many friends in the bathroom line, or in the bathroom. It's extremely intimate. You've let someone in.*

Full toilet paper text from *I put these words in the bathroom because the bathroom is a place where people read.*

In the bathroom, I tell Tamar that I have boundary issues. I mean this in the context of saying no. Although what is a boundary if not a certain type of refusal. This is where I end, in the context of you asking for things. This is where you end, too. An inquiry with unmet desire turns a question into a statement, and the questioner into a kind of thud. If we both agree that it's an ending, maybe it won't feel so bad. Then we can walk away.

There's so much we learn as we share a private space. At what point does overhearing become a form of engagement? *I've finished people's songs in the bathroom — where someone is in there, and I don't think they realize someone else is in there, and they start to sing a pop song, and I finish it. Not the entire song, but the chorus.*

In the bathroom, Trokon tells me that this is the first time he's been in this unisex space with a woman and felt comfortable. "I guess that means we're friends now," I suggest, and he agrees. The moment quickly passes, but I don't forget it.

At one point in high school, my friend and I were talking about how we wanted to get some Adderall after school. We were in a rebellious time in our lives. We walked out of the stall, and my teacher was right there. She wound up calling my parents to the school, and having a whole discussion with my parents. It ended up blowing over. It wasn't a big deal, but it was a scary moment. It was probably the most

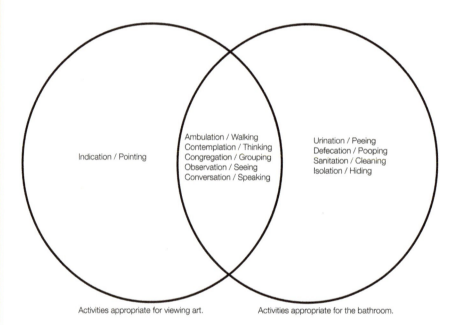

Indication / Pointing

Ambulation / Walking
Contemplation / Thinking
Congregation / Grouping
Observation / Seeing
Conversation / Speaking

Urination / Peeing
Defecation / Pooping
Sanitation / Cleaning
Isolation / Hiding

Activities appropriate for viewing art.   Activities appropriate for the bathroom.

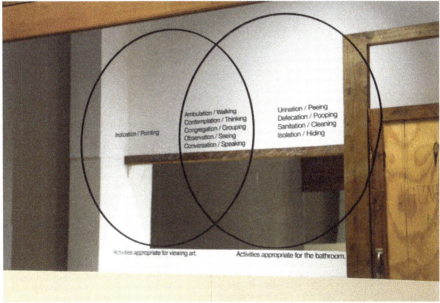

Indication / Pointing

Ambulation / Walking
Contemplation / Thinking
Congregation / Grouping
Observation / Seeing
Conversation / Speaking

Urination / Peeing
Defecation / Pooping
Sanitation / Cleaning
Isolation / Hiding

Activities appropriate for viewing art.

Activities appropriate for the bathroom.

As installed at the Knockdown Center, 2018.

Ribbons measuring spatial distances:
public, social, personal, and intimate.

CHAPTER FIVE:

PROTECT

& PRESERVE

Protect & Preserve

QUESTION:

What is the relationship
between people and safe places?

Protect & Preserve investigates the paired
relationship between a person and a city,
particularly focusing on the idea of safety. I
met with St. Louis residents in the location
of their choice: a place that felt particularly
and importantly safe. During our meetings, we
did two things: conducted a photoshoot of the
participant in his/her/their safe place; and
engaged in a brief conversation about safety,
focusing on the following questions:

    Do you feel safe?
    What is safety to you?
    What is safety to St. Louis?
    If you could talk to someone else
      about being safe, who would it be?
    What would you say?
    How would you talk about it?

These photographs and interviews became the
material for a postcard book. The project
premiered alongside a performance-lecture
about safety and empathy.

Chapter Five originally premiered at the
Pulitzer Arts Foundation for the St. Louis
Small Press Expo, and was produced with project
and residency support from the Luminary, and
financial support from the Rema Hort Mann
Foundation.

WHEN:

July - August 2016

WHERE:

St. Louis, MO

In July 2016, I met with St. Louis residents in the place of their choice: a place that felt particularly and importantly safe. During our meetings, we did two things: first, we engaged in a conversation about safety, focusing on the following questions:

Do you feel safe? Where do you feel safe? If you could talk to someone else about being safe, who would it be? What would you say? How would you talk about it?

Second, I conducted a photoshoot of the participant in his/her/ their safe place. The photos in this book were taken just after emotionally intimate interviews.

Participants have been identified in the way they specified: some people wished to include a job title, some a short description, and some no information other than name.

The chapter's title, Protect & Preserve, is a riff on the police motto: "To protect and to serve." It also serves as a reminder of what we all, as citizens, must do in order to maintain our communities.

PACIA ELAINE, POET

Literally once every year, every year and a half, I would move somewhere. My friends would call it the Pacia Itch. Sometimes I would get mad at something that was happening in St. Louis, and I would be itching, thinking *I need to get out of here.* So the fact that I really love this place says a lot for me. The fact that I find safety in this place says a lot for me. Because in the midst of storms, I'm prone to just move away from the storm.

COLE LU, QUEER IDENTIFIED VISUAL ARTIST

I wasn't exposed to extreme danger before. Maybe it was a luxury, being privileged, being protected. Sometimes I'm disgusted by how privileged I am. I look back at the history of my adolescence and think *oh, that was extremely privileged to live in an environment that provides that kind of safety.* So initially when I got this invitation, I thought, *am I qualified to talk about safety, though?*

Safety is multiple things. Safety is being able to have peace, and being able to relax mentally, emotionally. Safety is also physically not being in danger. I think about that question from the perspective of a former police officer. Unfortunately, or fortunately, that experience continues to cloud my mind and shape who I am. The idea of safety shapes everything that I do.

ALLISON C. ROLLINS

When I think of what place I feel safest as a Black woman, I think often it's hard even to feel safe in my own body, in the space that I inhabit. I definitely feel as a Black woman outside of my home, the level of access to safety that I have is very limited, and always a negotiation. I know how I think I'm representing myself in this space, but I don't know what you're seeing.

Safety is never having to say you're sorry. So if you're allowed to say things, do things, make mistakes, take risks, and you do it in a way that you think is ethical, responsible, legal, moral, whatever, and other people accept it even if they don't like it, you can be safe. And that implies responsibility on both sides, I think. Because if you're going to be safe, you have responsibility for others to help them feel safe. How you see yourself, how you see others, how you see others seeing you, and if you want to go one step further, how you see others seeing you see them. If you can slow yourself down long enough to go through that process, everyone can be safe, I think.

CARL PHILLIPS, POET & PROFESSOR OF ENGLISH

More than safety, sometimes people just don't want to encounter anything that reminds them that their fantasy of the world is not true.

Safety for St. Louis is unity. And that's the only word that popped into my mind: unity. As they say, a house divided can't stand. And the sooner people realize that we're all in the same situation — granted, Black people are getting the blunt end, and have been for some time — but there are also other people of color and even Whites who still struggle under the same oppressive system. So I think a safe space for us is unity. If you look at these branches, if I took one branch, you could snap it very easily. If I took 30 of those branches, varying in size, weight, and dimension, you could still break it, but it would be a little more difficult to do so.

NYKIA, DANCE TEAM MEMBER, 13 YEARS OLD

I think safety in St. Louis isn't violence. They think violence can solve every single issue. They think guns, or hand violence, or verbal violence, that any type of violence, any weapon or physical violence, they think that can fix everything. But really it can't, because the impact — it will create more violence later on in life.

Safety is subjective. We're so accustomed to defending the city, and it just depends on where you're from, or your frame of reference.

DANIELLE MCCOY, HALF OF WORK PLAY

As far as St. Louis, I don't know if people realize how much mental trauma we've been going through lately, for years. For decades. For generations. Even just talking and listening to stories from my grandparents, my great-grandparents, they don't want to talk about the past. I love stories. When I read a story about my people, and it's something really traumatic, it breaks my soul. People realize the trauma that they're putting other people through, with videos and articles and tweets and Facebook so readily in front of us, and it kind of screws us up inside. I cry. Water I look at as a purification. When I feel like I'm in water, I feel purified.

I often do not feel safe. And I think part of that is because I am an activist and an organizer. I am a queer woman. I am a young queer woman of color. It's the quadruple minority status that makes me afraid in a city like this that is experiencing so much tension and so much division. The fact that we sometimes can't see the intersectionality of our own struggles makes me feel unsafe because I live in those intersections.

If the patrolmen are subtle, not so much of a jerk, to where they are causing harassment rather than peace and surveillance, this would in turn make their district feel more safe. The district and the neighborhood would know that if there's a concern between neighbor and neighbor, or someone out of the neighborhood, that this offer would address the issue with a teacher's hand, with a father's hand, more so than with an officer's hand, which could possibly be seen as a threat for gaining or obtaining authority in the wrong manner.

The definition of safety has to change. If you're not safe, you're not safe. If I'm not safe, you're not safe.

KEN FLEISCHMAN, BORN AND RAISED IN ST. LOUIS

How would safety happen? We need some leadership, and I'm not seeing it at the national level in our politics — the presidential race. I don't know where it's going to come from, but there's a part of my soul that's saying, it's got to be grassroots. It's got to take people like you, and me, and other people to try to come together to do something profound. And this time around I feel like the issues are really complex. So. We need leadership, and right now we're kind of, as a nation, very divided, and floundering. I have to figure out what can I do about something like this. And obviously it starts simply, but something bigger needs to happen. I hope people start to try to find love and start the conversation.

I would write to my little cousin about safety. I would tell her if anyone puts hands on her, or if she is going to do something not safe, she needs to talk to somebody. Before she does something unsafe or really bad. Because she doesn't know what the other person might do back to her.

NANCY MORROW-HOWELL, PROFESSOR OF GERONTOLOGY, WASHINGTON UNIVERSITY SCHOOL OF SOCIAL WORK

I did focus groups with older adults who lived in Ferguson and surrounding areas about a year after the incident with the shooting of Michael Brown. And they were still feeling not safe. The African-American folks had a very long and engrained fear about the police, but they had developed a new fear about police non-intervention. Older adults, White folks and Black folks, witnessed where they thought the police in an older day, in a previous time, would have stepped in and intervened, but there was some more restraint, there was some more not being clear how to be involved — so they were afraid of the police, and they were afraid of not the police, if you know what I mean.

Find someone that you know is going to have your back no matter what happens. Someone that you know you can be safe with, rather than someone that someone else says you can be safe with. A designated safety area is different than someone that you personally know will help you.

JEFF VINES, CO-CREATOR OF STL STYLE

For me, getting out of my comfort zone actually makes me feel more safe, and more a part of the city. So I tend to explore areas that I'm not as familiar with, and change up my commutes. It makes you realize what a big city St. Louis actually is. Having a sense of adventure is safe for me.

We're taught to think in these terms, especially in St. Louis city, of neighborhoods, and segregation, and this is where all the White people are, this is where all the Black people are, this is sort of the Hispanic area. So I think the more we learn to cross over those borders and kind of step outside of our own world, the more accessible safety becomes. Because when we're not all strangers, we're just friends looking out for one another. There's nothing to fear anymore.

REBECCA RADFORD, STOREFRONT LEADER AT 10TH LIFE

Safety is, to me, a work. A work in progress. It never stops.

I think safety involves going out, getting out, knowing things, finding things, being a participant observer, being a volunteer. If you're always doing something until you've got yourself worn out, you're probably safe. People make you safe.

(This lecture-performance originally premiered at the Pulitzer Arts Foundation in October 2016. It has since been performed at the Weeksville Heritage Center in Brooklyn, NY, and at Washington & Lee University in Lexington, VA. The performance is accompanied by a slideshow. Indications for the slide transitions have been left as part of the script. Some of the slide images appear in this book. Others do not.)

[Slide #1: Title]

Hi. Hello. Thank you for coming.

My name is Chloë Bass. I'm an artist. I was born and raised in New York City. I live in Brooklyn now. I am thirty-three years old. I am a mixed race Black American.

I'm glad you're here.

[Slide #2: Credits]

This is *The Book of Everyday Instruction,* Chapter Five: *Protect & Preserve. The Book of Everyday Instruction* is my ongoing project about one-on-one social interaction. It has eight chapters in total. Each chapter of the project has its own title, focus, and central inquiry question.

If you've been in the gallery, you've seen some of the material from all eight chapters. The titles and questions appear as an element of wall text. The odd-numbered chapters (1, 3, 5, and 7) are conducted as social practice projects, directly engaging with others. Each of these chapters was produced in conjunction with a community in a historically important African-American city: Cleveland, Ohio (Chapter One); Greensboro, North Carolina (Chapter Three); St. Louis, Missouri (Chapter Five); and New Orleans, Louisiana (Chapter Seven). Even-numbered chapters (2, 4, 6, and 8) were produced as studio projects, although many of these chapters had ultimate manifestations in social spaces including shared restrooms, lecture halls, public gathering places, or even online.

For example: here we are in a lecture hall, and some of the work is also in your restrooms down the hall.

[Slide #3: Photo of Pacia]

This chapter, Chapter Five, investigates the relationship between people and safe spaces as a kind of partnership. The chapter's title, *Protect & Preserve*, is a riff off of the Los Angeles Police Department's motto, "to protect and to serve," which has been adopted by other police departments nationwide.

[Slide #4: Baton Rouge black and white photo.]

On January 11th, 2016, I started a document on my computer and titled it "Keep Yourself Safe." The date turned out to be significant for reasons that I won't be telling you now.

On July 7th, 2016, I landed in St. Louis. I had been invited by two great organizations, the Pulitzer Arts Foundation (a large non-profit institution) and the Luminary (a small artist-run residency program and gallery), to produce new work in response to their city. I flew to St. Louis from New Orleans, where just days beforehand, Alton Sterling had been killed by police in Baton Rouge.

I had never been to St. Louis before.

[Slide #5: Photo of Natalie]

I did not (necessarily) go to St. Louis to do a project about race. But there are certain things that are unavoidable. Last summer was a slap in the face. There wasn't a single day when I woke up feeling anything other than the sense that I was drowning.

[Slide #6: Photo of Joy]

I want to tell you about how this all happened.

I am an artist who works responsively. Often, this comes to mean that I make my work through conversation.

In St. Louis, I had the opportunity to speak with twenty-two strangers: friends of the Pulitzer Arts Foundation (one of the major St. Louis-based arts organizations, and the commissioner of this project), friends of the Luminary (a non-profit residency and studio program), and friends of the first set of interviewees, about safety.

[Slide #7: Photo of Carl]

I asked each of my participants six questions:

1. I asked if we could meet in a place that is safe to you. Can you tell me where we are and why you picked this place?

2.What is safety to you?

3. What is safety to St. Louis?

4. If you could write a letter to someone else about safety right now, who would you write to and what would you say?

5. Finish the sentence: "Safety is . . ."

6. Is there anything that you did not get to say because of what I asked, or the way that I asked it?

[Slide #8: Photo of De]

I like speaking to people directly for a lot of reasons. There's something very nice about being held together in the deep, magical space that can exist between two people. The conversations I had ranged from 10 minutes to 90.

[Slide #9: Photo of Rebecca]

I met people in parks, in their homes, in their workplaces. I met people on street corners. I met Rebecca at Tenth Life Cat Rescue, where she is a volunteer. Making safe space for others helps her to feel safe herself. I asked everyone my six questions, and in the process I learned about their families, their lives in the past and present, and so much more.

[Slide #10: Photo of Steenz]

For me, taking a stranger to a safe place and having a conversation about safety is really odd and anxiety-provoking. It's essential to make sure that the best parts of that oddness are preserved and turned into something productive. At the same time, I have to work hard to make myself extra comfortable for the person who's allowing for this vulnerable interaction to happen. Balancing these kinds of dynamics is a huge part of my craft.

[Slide #11: Photo of Nancy]

Most people I spoke with fell into one of two camps:

1. Safety requires the presence of others. We are safe when we are together.

OR.

2. We can only be safe if we are alone.

[Slide #12: Baton Rouge iconic photo of a woman standing up to riot cops]

We know this image.

Iconic photographs of civil rights actions tend to emphasize one of two things: either that we are not safe in the presence of The Other; or that we are only safe when bolstered by others. No wonder that we learn so little through the picture alone.

[Slide #13: Photo of Kevin]

My photos were meant to convey not the single snapshot (which they are, in a way, although I don't think I should tell you how many images I took in order to capture 22 moments of calm), but rather the sense of the ongoing: the safe space as a space that holds bodies in repose. Where taking the photograph a moment (or two, or five moments) later would actually not produce a totally different image.

[Slide #14: Photo of little boy and police]

Are we safer when we're allowed to maintain a certain type of innocence, or are we safer when we can't? What's better, privilege, or awareness?

[Slide #15: Photo of Cole]

Cole told me that she felt unqualified to talk about safety. She had grown up in a safe place, she said. She had had experiences that she knew other people never had the chance to have. But she also spoke of the difficult of being away from her family. Because she is always alone, she said, she has to make herself very safe. Always. She spoke to me a lot about control. In the meantime, she let me frame her. She let me record her voice. She allowed her image to be up to me.

[Slide #16: Photo of Randy]

I used to think of family as a kind of nesting, a concept by which everything can be neatly contained within a single structure.

[Slide #17: Photo of Jeff]

In a nested system, obligation to others holds each of us in our place. This is the regularity against which we rail in adolescence (and, often, beyond).

[Slide #18: Photo of I Am A Man]

But in truth the idea of family is fraught, temporary. Wayne Koestenbaum, in his book Notes on Glaze, writes about "the frozenness of being in the wrong body at the wrong time and in the wrong place." What happens when that wrong body joins others, makes bonds, becomes family? What happens when we are so many wrong bodies together?

[Slide #19: Photo of water hose trained on Black protestors]

The impermanence of family could reference any number of conditions: the ways in which families can be chosen, not born-into; the families we leave; the impossible world that sends dad to work in the car and brings him home only as another victim on the evening news. What does father mean then?

[Slide #20: Photo of Dani]

One thing that came up during my conversations was the weary heaviness of ongoing trauma. Danielle talked to me openly about this. She told me, "As far as St. Louis, I don't know if people realize how much mental trauma we've been going through lately, for years. For decades. For generations. Even just talking and listening to stories from my grandparents, my great-grandparents, they don't want to talk about the past. I love stories. When I read a story about my people, and it's something really traumatic, it breaks my soul. People realize the trauma that they're putting other people through with videos and articles and tweets and Facebook so readily in front of us, and it kind of fucks us up inside. I cry. Water I look at as a purification. When I feel like I'm in water, I feel purified."

[Slide #21: Photo of Silas]

I want to make something beautiful as a pathway to discussing something difficult. This is not a remedy. It's just another kind of door into receiving what we need. Silas told me if I kept moving until I was exhausted, I'd be safe. He advised me that the best way to explore St. Louis would be on roller skates. But somehow I wanted to find safety in stillness.

[Slide #22: Photo of Racially Profiled Sweatshirt]

I think a lot about the attitudes of safety enacted — and avoided — by those who are able to march, and keep marching. Make no mistake: the conditions of ongoing protest are special. Our needs change. Our need for each other changes. Is the safety in the gathering, or in the staying home? When my Black mother calls and tells me not to protest, I know that it is due to a sense that my body is hers, which it is. If my body were not hers, the urgency to march would be much less.

[Slide #23: Photo of Alison]

What does it mean to feel safe as a body? Alison talked to me about the safety of the mind, about safety as a condition that we hold internally, but admitted to me that as a Black female body in the world, she almost never felt safe. Alison called safety a negotiation. It's interesting when we feel our safety lies outside of ourselves, that safety comes from the permission of others. It's interesting, but also scary.

[Slide #24: Photo of Stay Woke shirt]

The day I flew to St. Louis, I was wearing a sweatshirt that read "UNARMED CIVILIAN." As I was going through security, worried that I was going to miss my flight, a TSA officer from the lane opposite mine gestured to me. He indicated the front of my chest and I looked down, wondering what security rule I was violating. When I looked up, confused, he mouthed to me, "I really like your shirt."

[Slide #25: Photo of Con]

Con told me that she refuses to live like she's not safe. It was not my job to question this. She went on to talk to me about the responsibility of helping other people feel safe, of how safety is something that we share. Like the way I think of my work, she positioned safety as a kind of dialogue. Who would you talk to? What would you say?

[Slide #26: Photo of Eugene]

I grew up singing Civil Rights songs without knowing what they were. We met in assembly every Friday morning, pledged allegiance to the flag, and then shrieked our way through We Shall Overcome, elementary-school style. No one told us the history. Yet there was never a point where the message was far from us, either.

[Slide #27: Photo of Nykia]

Still, there's a difference between proximity, and immediacy. Nykia talked to me about her neighborhood, and how violence only begets more violence. She is thirteen years old, in the 8th grade, and a member of her school's dance team. She is quick to answer questions, and likes to pretend she's a television reporter so she can get more gossip from people. This should be enough. Why can't just this be enough for one girl's life?

[Slide #28: Photo of *Am I Next*]

Twice that summer in St. Louis, I was riding in the car with a relative stranger, having a terrific conversation on the surface, and all the while thinking, "if the police pull us over and something happens, I will not know how to save you." Thinking, "we should both just get out of this car. It doesn't matter where we need to go."

I probably don't have to tell you that both of the nice strangers I was riding with were Black.

[Slide #29: Photo of Michael Allen]

The philosopher George Yancy talks about expanding the idea of who we call our neighbors. This seems really different to me than expanding the idea of what we call our neighborhoods. We are somehow able to think about space without people. This, to me, is the opposite of urban living. The space and the people become inseparable. When we sign on for one, we sign up for both. Michael walked me up and down Chippewa Street, talking to me about safety as social connection. It was a very hot day. We barely saw a soul.

[Slide #30: Photo of die-in]

Here's a thought experiment: before you go outside each day, turn yourself into a ghost story. Really mean it. Will that serve to keep you more alive, or less?

[Slide #31: Photo of Terrell]

This is the only person who asked to meet me not in the place where he feels safest, but where he has thought the most about safety. As a very young man, and as a very young father, Terrell Carter was a beat cop on Cherokee Street. We walked the street and talked about policing as reactive, not proactive. Then we talked about the importance of safety as a family man. He's not an officer anymore.

[Slide #32: Photo of tank coming]

We need to learn that in most cases, "we are family" means nothing more or less than "until I can't recognize you in the dark." There's a point where you think being around other people will help. And there's a point where it obviously doesn't.

[Slide #33: Photo of multiple protest signs]

Something's got to give. Maybe it's us. Maybe we can continue to give and give and give. Even in the face of failure, giving retains some kind of meaning. Even when we're told that we have nothing, this is one way to discover that in fact, we have a lot.

[Slide #34: Photo of Gaitor]

One person who I talked to, Gaitor Redd, told me a long story. I don't remember all the details, but the gist was that one good turn begets another. The ending of the story was a shared home cooked supper made by a formerly hateful lady, resulting in the sale of a recipe and profits and fame for a local community. I haven't figured out how to create safety, but I feel pretty good about that.

[Slide #35: Photo of Ken]

There's always an edge of unsafety around any kind of safety. Being aware of that edge is what keeps you safe. But that means we're also always thinking about potentially not being safe.

Maybe, like Ken, it means that we're offering continued prayers for our safety, and the safety of others. He told me he's praying for leadership, even as he knows the responsibility lies with us.

[Slide #36: Flag photo]

At some point we have to admit this is our day, this is our city, this is our life. It's not what comes next. It's now.

[Slide #37: Rainbow photo]

Look, I took the time to make this beautiful for you. I took the time to put it all down. The question now is what you're going to do with it. The question now is how we're going to live.

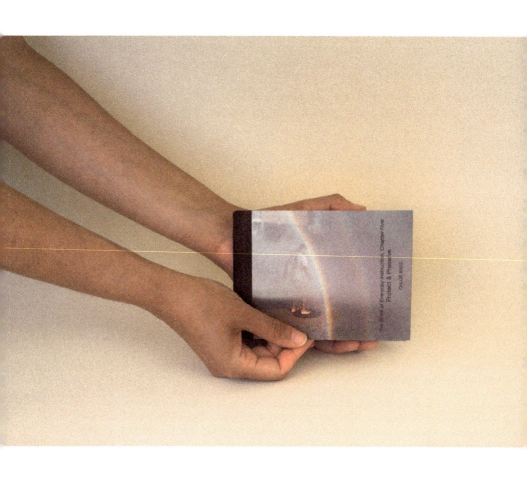

Documentation image of the *Protect & Preserve* postcard book.

CHAPTER SIX:

WHAT IS SHARED,

WHAT IS OFFERED

What is shared, what is offered

How do we share love between individuals and institutions?

What is shared, what is offered focuses on the pairing between individuals and institutions as a form of attachment and attention that's akin to love. Structured as a meal in four courses (engagement, maintenance, romance, and healing), the work offers conceptual pairings and blends to guide participants past a scarcity mentality of emotional economy. The chapter's title is borrowed from Michel de Certeau's *The Practice of Everyday Life*, in the chapter "Bread and Wine." De Certeau describes the relationship between bread, wine, and the social economies produced between dinner guests, as follows: "Wine contains, as a result of the unique virtues attributed to it through a social consensus, a motivating social force that bread does not have: the latter is shared, wine is offered."

Chapter Six consists of a series of four diagrammatic photos representing different phases of love, a corresponding scent installation involving spices, a couples-counseling workshop for individuals and institutions, and a series of five conversations centered around an image-sharing game.

Chapter Six originally premiered at CUE Art Foundation (photos and couples counseling), Franklin Street Works (tableware), and Independent Curators International (conversation series).

December 2016 - February 2018

New York, NY

FACING PAGE: *The Four Phases of Love: Nobody Loves Me* (top),
The Impossible Fairytale (bottom), 2017.

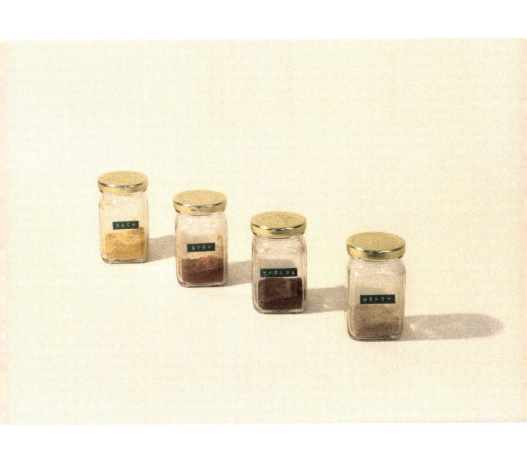

FACING PAGE: *The Four Phases of Love: We tried to love each other but it didn't work out* (top), *I love someone but it's not requited* (bottom), 2017. ABOVE: detail view of spice jar installation.

The Four Phases of Love as installed at CUE Art Foundation, 2017.

The conversation series for *What is shared, what is offered* began with me sending each of my guests a private love letter, which included an invitation to join me for an evening at Independent Curators International.

After accepting my initial invitation, each guest received the following instructions:

> *First, I'm so glad that you and I will be sharing this time. I really look forward to being in discussion with you.*
>
> *Second, I want to talk to you a bit about the format of the event. Since it will just be the two of us (plus someone from ICI as our interlocutor), I was hoping we could play a small game. As you know, I want to speak with you about intimacy over time. I am also interested to speak about [topic varies by guest], which should come as no surprise.*
>
> *Here is the game: we will each put together a series of 5 - 10 images (you can choose the final number, and I will match it; remember that if you choose 10 we will have 20 in total) that will guide our conversation. We will not look at each others' images before the event. During the event, we will each have a chance to respond to the image the other person put forward, and then to speak about it together. We will do this until all images have been discussed, or time runs out, whichever comes first.*
>
> *The images can come from anywhere: preferably not your own work, but other artworks, news media, found things, the world. Let me know how this sounds to you. My hope is that this kind of instinctive conversation will guide us towards a more genuine conversation and larger truths. Remember: intimacy is the goal.*

Please meet me on the evening of February 14th, 2017. Independent Curators International, our partner, has committed to providing the following: a warm space for our gathering, a loving audience of witnesses, and wine and chocolate for all.

It would be my honor to spend a few hours with you, sharing our thoughts on the following questions: *how do we remain together, scaling intimacy over time? What do we learn in the service of change?*

Dear Doug,

I believe in the power of many scales of love. Sometimes *for a day* is no less significant than *for a lifetime*. What is a lifetime if not a succession of hours that we endow with meaning (sometimes during; often after)?

Here's way to think about time: there are moments when the body insists. But tastes change, and formulating a different relationship to time feels urgent to our survival. If we don't engage with the nastier side of intimacy (a finger up the asshole can result in shit on the sheets), we will never know the real work of understanding one another.

Forgive me if you find this crude. I'm making a point about how we love. I want our knowledge to come together in the service of the future. One danger of nostalgia is that certain images are so embedded in black and white, it becomes impossible to remember that they were originally lived in color.

I admire your life and work deeply. I hope you can join me. It will be warm.

Yours,
Chloë

Please meet me on the evening of June 8th, 2017. Independent Curators International, our partner, has committed to providing the following: a friendly space for our gathering, a loving audience of witnesses, and wine and popcorn for all.

It would be my honor to spend a few hours with you, sharing our thoughts on the following questions: *what do we allow with our displeasure? When do acts of refusal become exquisite?*

Dear Bill,

Most of my best work happens via correspondence. When I run out of correspondence, I'm not sure what to do. Yet I also find myself exhausted by the demands of other people, the consistent presence that accompanies being in the world.

It's in this stubborn insistence of needing to be always with others, yet finding that others never please me, that I hope we can meet.

The failure to be pleased is not a failure to find pleasure. To make anything this simple is a mistake. We will never be cool until our minds become still and clean. I don't want anaesthetized grappling. There's a world beyond growth, and what we find there may be horrific in its appeal.

Everything I've ever touched remains with me, for better and for worse. I am sick from it. I am sick, and deeply engaged.

I admire your life and work deeply. I hope you can join me. It will be fresh.

Yours,
Chloë

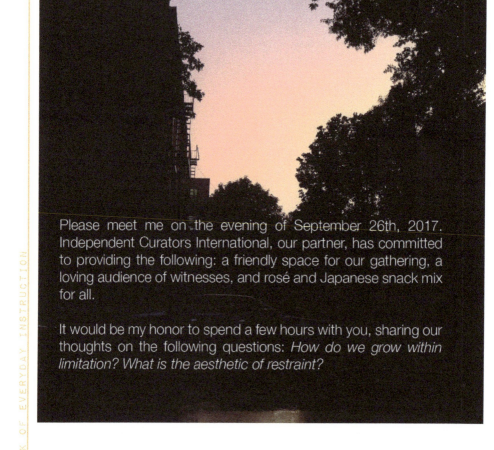

Please meet me on the evening of September 26th, 2017. Independent Curators International, our partner, has committed to providing the following: a friendly space for our gathering, a loving audience of witnesses, and rosé and Japanese snack mix for all.

It would be my honor to spend a few hours with you, sharing our thoughts on the following questions: *How do we grow within limitation? What is the aesthetic of restraint?*

Dear Tiona,

When I say I believe in magic, what I mean is, *will you go with me to a place I haven't made yet*? Of all things, the heartbeat is both the smallest and the most amazing. To understand it is a dangerous compulsion: to take a heart into your own hands is, in many cases, to elimiate its beat. In other words, both capture and naming can be profound forms of loss.

In the face of this knowledge, I'm curious about what holds us together. It may be as easy as coffee in the morning with someone you love, discussing things you both appreciate. A job well done. A good night's sleep. A story saved for later. There's a certain kind of minimalism that points us towards potential. A whispered suggestion constitutes the grounds of an invitation in a way that more baroque structures never will.

I am stuck between the comfort of believing that everything I've written is true, and the ongoing desire for more.

I admire your life and work deeply. I hope you can join me. It will be open.

Yours,
Chloë

55 GLEN DELI GROC

Please meet me on the evening of November 14th, 2017. Independent Curators International, our partner, has committed to providing the following: a friendly space for our gathering, a loving audience of witnesses, and wine and gluten free snacks for all.

It would be my honor to spend a few hours with you, sharing our thoughts on the following questions: *what is the role of play during conditions of emergency? How can we change the ways we learn?*

Dear Lisi,

Neither you nor I work with children. It's also been a long time since I was a child, although in many ways my younger self feels closer to me than she has in years. Regardless: I think we're both familiar with the great capacity of play. Games, for so much of our early lives, are the sincerest form of learning. It's not that children are better than adults because of their innocence. It's because for the child, to whom everything is new, the only rational response to everyday circumstances is contintually to question them.

Here's a question I can't shed: in these times of deep distress, how do we play? One thing that continues to astound me is that life goes on. It was only on November 9th that I walked onto crowded subway cars and experienced muffled mass weeping. Even as we integrate protest into a regular roster of post-brunch activities, there is something larger that remains true: we cannot help but do our day to day. I fear the emergency that lies beyond the insistent possbilities of daily life, but cannot say what it might be.

I admire your life and work deeply. I hope you can join me. It will be open.

Yours,
Chloë

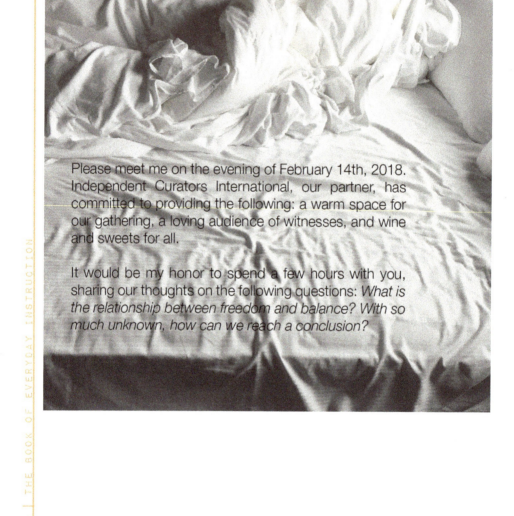

Please meet me on the evening of February 14th, 2018. Independent Curators International, our partner, has committed to providing the following: a warm space for our gathering, a loving audience of witnesses, and wine and sweets for all.

It would be my honor to spend a few hours with you, sharing our thoughts on the following questions: *What is the relationship between freedom and balance? With so much unknown, how can we reach a conclusion?*

Dear Jess,

I try to invent rituals that impose a kind of regularity on two assumedly solid, but quite abstract, phenomena: first, myself; and second, time. I consider this a form of holding. No matter how old we get, we always need the swaddle. Perhaps what is meant by *cradle to grave* is that nothing is certain but boundaries.

You asked me recently, "What does it mean to reject relationships of equal exchange not because of any malicious intent, but because it might mean a restructuring of how we consider power and care?" This is a good question. It suggests there may be ample room for dialogue within the unfair. And the unfair is a permanent condition.

I am trying to be crazy, but in a good way. I wonder about the relationship between *freedom* and *balance*. Walking enthusiastically, I fell on my face in front of you. I felt neither shame, nor surprise. Acceptance of what is can be a form of invitation. Come in. Be warm. So much is still unknown.

I admire your life and work deeply. I hope you can join me. This is the end.

Yours,
Chloë

Doug Ashford is an artist, teacher and writer based in New York. He is Associate Professor at The Cooper Union where he has taught sculpture, design, and interdisciplinary studies since 1989. Ashford's principle visual practice from 1982 to 1996 was the multi-form practice of Group Material, whose work has been recently compiled in the book Show and Tell: A Chronicle of Group Material (Four Corners Books, 2010). Since 1996 he has continued to produce paintings, essays and collaborative projects that engage sociality with artistic form. His most recent public effort ended in the project Who Cares (Creative Time, 2006), a book built from a series of conversations between Ashford and other cultural practitioners on public expression, ethics, and beauty. Recent exhibitions of his paintings include "Abstract Possible", Tensta Konsthall and other locations (2010-12), dOCUMENTA 13, Kassel (2012) and the Gwangju Bienalle 11(2016). A collection of essays, Doug Ashford: Writings and Conversation, (Mousse Publishing, 2013), was published on the occasion of his retrospective exhibition at the Grazer Kunstverein that year. He is represented by Wilfried Lentz Rotterdam.

Bill Dietz is a composer and writer, based since 2003 in Berlin. From sounding the facade of Le Corbusier's Unité d'habitation in Marseille to orchestrating echoes across city blocks in Manhattan, his work traces genealogies of publicness and the performance of listening. He is co-chair of Music/Sound in Bard College's MFA program, and is currently Guest Professor of Sound at the Academy of Media Arts in Cologne. With Woody Sullender he co-founded and edits Ear | Wave | Event. In 2015 Edition Solitude released a monograph on his "Tutorial Diversions," and in Fall 2017 a book accompanying his work L'école de la claque will appear.

Tiona Nekkia McClodden is a visual artist, filmmaker, and curator whose work explores, and critiques issues at the intersections of race, gender, sexuality and social commentary. McClodden's interdisciplinary approach traverses documentary film, experimental video, sculpture, and sound installations. Themes explored in McClodden's films and works have been re-memory and more recently narrative biomythography.

Since 1998, Lisi Raskin has traveled to remote locations
exploring the intersection of nuclear-age fears and utopian
mythologies as they manifest in oral histories and the
architectures of the Cold War. Raskin's on-site research has
informed the making of paintings, drawings, objects, videos,
and large, constructed environments that she has exhibited
internationally. Slowly but surely, Raskin's installations
have become laboratories where the artist deliberately
builds bridges between politicized subject matter, utopian
architecture, abstraction, collaborative making, non-
hierarchical interventions into normative systems of power,
and radical pedagogy. Her web projects have been published
in Triple Canopy magazine, with The Dia Foundation, and on
Creative Time Global Reports. She has built large-scale
environments at the 11th International Istanbul Biennale,
the 2nd Athens Biennale, and the 3rd Singapore Biennale. She
has installed site-sensitive sound projects in the 1st Time
Machine Biennale of Contemporary Art, D-O Ark Underground
and the Momentum 7 Biennale of Nordic Art. Raskin was born in
Miami, Florida. She received her BA in Fine Arts from Brandeis
University and her MFA from Columbia University. She has
been the recipient of numerous awards and grants including
a Creative Time Global Residency Grant, the Guna S Mundheim
Berlin Prize at the American Academy in Berlin, among others.
Raskin is currently department head of Sculpture at RISD
and a member of the rock band Da Peeblz. With this group,
she is working on an intersectional, feminist, children's
propaganda album.

Jessica Lynne is co-founder and editor of ARTS.BLACK, a journal of art criticism from Black perspectives. She received her B.A. in Africana Studies from NYU and has been awarded residencies and fellowships from Art21 and The Cue Foundation, Callaloo, and The Center for Book Arts. Her writing has appeared in publications such as Aperture, Art in America, The Brooklyn Rail, and Kinfolk. She is a Winter 2018 Columnist-in-Residence at Open Space and currently serves as the Manager of Development and Communication at Recess. She is co-editor, alongside Sharon Louden, of a forthcoming book about the art world that will be published by Intellect Ltd. and The University of Chicago Press.

This essay was originally commissioned by ARTS.BLACK for the 2017 Common Field Convening. It was published on Arts.Black, as well as by Common Field, in October 2017.

SORRY NOT SORRY.
(COUPLES COUNSELING FOR ARTISTS AND
INSTITUTIONS: STEP TWO)[1]

(Author's note: *In contemplating how our world holds us (or doesn't), I have been examining the role of apology. We seem to fear direct apology, perhaps because it sets a precedent for future reparations (i.e. if I say sorry now, how many times will I need to say sorry in the future?). Is apology a moment, a process, or a rut? How can we begin to see it as an opportunity?*

Sorry not sorry is an interweaving of personal experiences of apology, or the blank gaps of non-apology, mixed with quotes from famous institutional and professional apologies. Quotes appear in bold. The source of each quote has been cited in the footnotes. A database of political apologies and reparations can be found here: http://political-apologies.wlu.ca/index.php. Both the search function and the links to external sources only sometimes work. Sorry about that.

I recently apologized to someone myself, the real way: I acknowledged what had happened, I said it was because of me, and then I said the words I'm sorry. I also cried a little. As to that last bit, I wish I hadn't. Still, the vulnerability inherent even to the shabbiest of apologies makes it an interesting point of departure from which to dissect the relationship between individuals and institutions. -- Chloë Bass)

Apologies for mis-attributing your role in the project!
Apologies for the random reach-out.
Apologies for my delay here.
I apologize that I couldn't send an object up to Montreal.
Our apologies for the confusion.
Apologies for duplicate emails.
I apologize for not sending a clear and specific proposal.
Llamas to apologize to Texans now.[2]

---

1 *Presented as part of Chloë Bass' project* The Book of Everyday Instruction, Chapter Six: What is shared, what is offered. *Previous couples therapy sessions between artists and institutions have explored an exploration of phases of love shared over time ("Step One," which premiered in February 2017 at CUE Art Foundation as part of* The Visible Hand, *curated by David Xu Borgonjon), as well as couples counseling for individuals and their relationship to Blackness (which premiered at the Design Studio for Social Intervention in March 2017, a few days shy of Black History Month (sorry/not sorry), at the invitation of Kenneth Bailey.*

2 *A brief sampling of the first 50 search results for "apologize" in my Gmail inbox, as of September 25th, 2017.*

We did some homework—speaking to New Yorkers, branding people, and even running some survey work asking about the name and any potential offense it might cause. But it's clear that we may not have been asking the right questions of the right people. Despite our best intentions and our admiration for traditional bodegas, we clearly hit a nerve this morning, we apologize. Rather than disrespect to traditional corner stores—or worse yet, a threat—we intended only admiration. We commit to reviewing the feedback and understanding the reactions from today.[3]

Well-cited: the things that people say when they think everyone in the room is like them. Less-cited: the things they don't say when they realize that wasn't the case. I am made strange to myself through the apology of not passing and the silences it prompts.[4]

First, it should be said (I wish it went without saying) that no racial implication was intended, by Time or by the artist. One could argue that it is racist to say that blacker is more sinister, and some African Americans have taken that position in the course of this dispute, but that does not excuse insensitivity. To the extent that this caused offense to anyone, I deeply regret it. Nor did we intend any imputation of guilt. We were careful to avoid that in our story, but for at least some people, this cover picture was worth several thousand words. The issues surrounding photo-illustration, particularly with regard to news photos, are much more complex. To a certain extent, our critics are absolutely right: altering news pictures is a risky practice, since only documentary authority makes photography of any value in the practice of journalism. On the other hand, photojournalism has never been able to claim the transparent neutrality attributed to it. Photographers choose angles and editors choose pictures to make points[.][5]

---

3 *The start-up company Bodega's apology about their name, and general launch proceedings, to the people of the internet, 2017, accesed via [https://blog.bodega.ai/so-about-our-name-aa5bff63a92d].*

4 *a) While I have never, to my knowledge, been mistaken for white, I am often seen as not-Black even by other Black colleagues. Passing is complicated, so I do not expect an apology for these moments of misidentification, but I wonder what purpose it serves. [and/or] b) I tend to find myself in spaces where people share a fair amount of educational affiliation, so difference can come as quite a surprise.*

5 *Jim Gaines, then managing editor of TIME Magazine, apologizing for the infamous cover photo that darkened OJ Simpson's skin color, accessed via [http://www.thewrap.com/oj-fact-check-read-time-magazines-apology-for-making-simpson-blacker/].*

A sharing exercise at an outdoor art event in New York in July. It's a hot day, and I'm partnered with a stranger, a young white woman, to take turns holding each other's heavy places. I hold her first. My focus is hazy in the heat, but I breathe and try to accept her. After a few minutes, we're told to switch. I place my hands on top of her hands, gradually giving her the weight of my arms. She begins to tremble, adjusts herself, and then looks into my eyes with alarm.

I feel sick, she says, *I need to sit down.* She slumps, puts her head down: *I'm sorry.* I rub her back. *It's okay,* I think, *if I didn't have to feel the way I feel in the world, I wouldn't want to, either.*[6]

[T]hank you for caring enough to complain or to praise. Perhaps we can all agree that whatever values we look for in the theater, we all stand on the common ground that it is a vital and important art form that we look to to illuminate the human experience with complexity and integrity.[7]

Note the way we treat other people as vaults: *I told you to remember that so I wouldn't have to hold onto it myself.* I can't count the number of times some supposed ally has pointed me towards a piece of Black information -- even useful things I don't yet know -- only later to ask "wait, what's that?" when I reference that same information again. No sign of a blush for the fact that you gave me something so you had the permission to forget it yourself.[8]

We're sorry for the massive disruption it's caused their lives. There's no one who wants this over more than I do. I would like my life back.[9]

I was sitting on the floor of Powell's, reading Roxane Gay's *Hunger* and beating myself up for not choosing a more interesting book while surrounded by so many rare things, when I was struck by <u>a sudden sneezing</u> attack. Once, then twice, and on and on. No

6 *I tend to take no longer than 10 minutes between admitting I feel nauseated and actually vomiting.*

7 *Tim Stanford's apology to the audience of Playwrights Horizons, 2013, accessed via[https://mobile.nytimes.com/blogs/artsbeat/2013/03/25/the-flick-prompts-an-explanation-from-playwrights-horizons]*

8 *A corollary to this is when the information people are feeding me somehow corresponds to their sense that they've invented who I am, or suddenly been the first person to discover me out of nowhere. This is very much, I imagine, how America felt when Columbus sailed up and crowned it the Indies.*

9 *BP CEO Tony Hayward's apology to residents of the Gulf Coast following the 2010 oil spill, accessed via [http://www.cnn.com/2010/US/05/30/gulf. oil.spill/index.html]. An apology advertisement video can be viewed here: https://www.youtube.com/watch?v=_AwD_7yNzKo*

one near me said anything. My eyes began to swell. The sneezes continued. I believed I was cursed: to keep up these exhausting explosions until someone acknowledged me with *bless you.*[10]

I know that my public comments and my silence about this matter gave a false impression. I misled people, including even my wife. I deeply regret that.[11]

Every day, the weight of this work breaks my heart, and then I work again to unbreak it. Surely there must be more to life's labor than this.[12]

For those who were abused by a member of the clergy, I am deeply sorry for the times when you or your family spoke out, to report the abuse, but you were not heard or believed. Please know that the Holy Father hears you and believes you.[13]

In the importance of acknowledging context and how it holds us, let me tell you that I intended to write this work entirely in transit between Portland and New York City on September 11th, 2017. I liked this disconnected scene: imagining the *I'm sorrys* that tie me to the ground while floating disconnected through the air. But I couldn't do it. I was seated next to someone else's grandmother. We were traveling together. It is hard sitting down to a piece of writing when you're responsible for someone else's relative. It is even harder if you're responsible for your own. Your own relatives know when you're lying.[14]

The time has now come for the nation to turn a new page in Australia's history by righting the wrongs of the past and so moving forward with confidence to the future. We apologise for the laws and policies of successive Parliaments and governments that have inflicted profound grief, suffering and

---

10 *Fourteen sneezes, at which point I got up and moved.*

11 *Bill Clinton's apology to the American people concerning the nature of his relationship with Monica Lewinsky, 1998, accessed via [http://www.cnn.com/ALLPOLITICS/1998/08/17/speech/transcript.html].*

12 *First recorded instance of heartbreak: sometime in the fall of 1997, my 8th grade year. Cause: the senior boy I liked not saying hello to me during his travels from homeroom to science class (Physics? Chemistry?), a route that I strategically walked on as many mornings as time permitted. Later, when I was older, this boy became my boyfriend. We dated for over three years. When we separated, the heartbreak I felt was different, but not worse.*

13 *Pope Francis' apology for ongoing incidents of juvenile sexual abuse in the Catholic Church, 2014, accessed via [http://www.phillyvoice.com/transcript-pope-francis-apology-church-victims/].*

14 *Like many people, I lie more about innocuous things than important ones.*

loss on these our fellow Australians. We apologise especially for the removal of Aboriginal and Torres Strait Islander children from their families, their communities and their country. For the pain, suffering and hurt of these Stolen Generations, their descendants and for their families left behind, we say sorry. To the mothers and the fathers, the brothers and the sisters, for the breaking up of families and communities, we say sorry. And for the indignity and degradation thus inflicted on a proud people and a proud culture, we say sorry.[15]

I'm so sorry, he writes. *Please forgive me*. And I do.[16]

---

15 *Apology from the Australian government to the Aboriginal people of Australia, 2008, accessed via [http://www.australia.gov.au/about-australia/ our-country/our-people/apology-to-australias-indigenous-peoples].*

16 *A future iteration of this work may focus on forgiveness, and whether the equation of forgiveness = forgetting really holds true. Sometimes I think I forgive more when I remember the incident that required the apology. To re-member translates forgiveness into an ongoing act rather than a generosity that stops after its instance.*

What is shared, what is offered:
Maintenance, 2017, product documentation.

CHAPTER SEVEN:

SUBJECT TO

CHANGE

WITHOUT

NOTICE

Subject to change without notice

How do we recognize an ongoing coupling in spite of change?

Subject to change without notice returns to the relationship between people and the cities they live in, this time focusing on subjective experiences of color as a way to track and share public space. The chapter's title was taken from a line of text that appears on all historic and contemporary public transportation maps in New Orleans: subject to change without notice. This sentence also serves as a good description of urban life in the time of rampant gentrification: for the resident, local change often occurs without warning, request, or consideration—something that happens *to* rather than *with* a neighborhood.

Chapter Seven consists primarily of a free phone app, *City Palette*, which is available for iPhone and Android. Through camera and location access, City Palette allows users to upload the colors from their own local environment. The app will choose a dominant tone to save from each user-submitted image. Users assign their own names to the colors they upload, and can view 'nearby' swatches from other users. Allowing users to generate and name their own color-coded swatches of New Orleans (and other cities) will reflect and convey an individualized and experiential portrait of urban space—not just what they see, but how they see it.

Chapter Seven premiered at Antenna (New Orleans) as part of the Spillways Fellowship, and was produced with support from VIA Art Fund.

June 2016 - November 2017

New Orleans, LA

Howyoudoing?

CITY PALETTE is a photo and design app interpreting locations through color collections. So many cities are unique in their color spectrums: from the tropical hues of Miami Beach to the stately grays of London, colors are an important way to interpret where we are. City Palette was first designed for use in New Orleans, Louisiana, a historically colorful city in the midst of many changes.

ADD YOUR OWN COLOR

Through camera and location access, City Palette allows users to upload the colors from their own local environment. The app will choose a dominant tone to save from each user-submitted image. Users assign their own names to the colors they upload. Have you ever wanted to name your own crayon? Now's your chance.

SEE YOUR CITY'S COLORS

Users can browse other "nearby" colors to see how people near them are seeing things. Colors can be arranged into downloadable collections appropriate for use with most design software.

DOWNLOAD THE APP

Available for iOS through the iTunes Store or Android through the Google Play Store.

Original bus ads for *City Palette* in New Orleans, Louisiana.

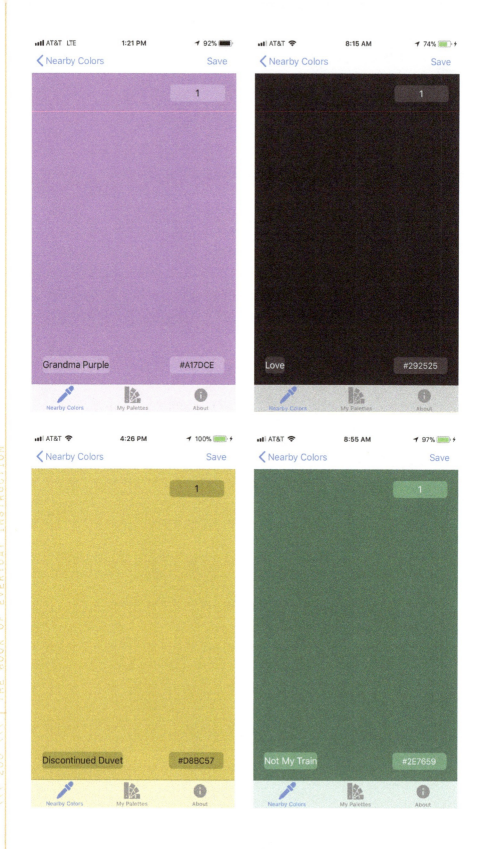

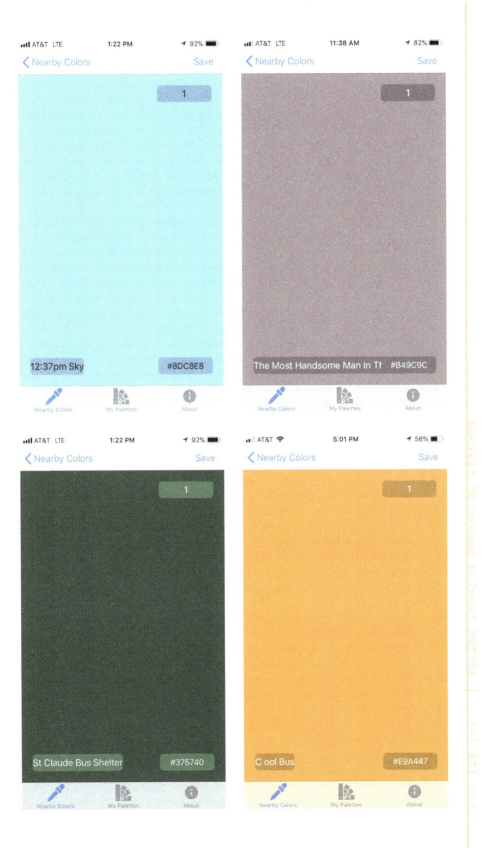

I've been in New Orleans collecting colors, a selection of which are presented on these pages as the beginning of an answer to something. Later, I'll be releasing these colors as a certain kind of narrative about people, and transit, and the ways our cities support us and let us down, but that's not fixed yet.

For now, let's say this: colors are associative ideas. They're placeholders for something we remember but can't quite approach. If this sounds romantic, it is. New Orleans is a romantic place. But I mean something particular when I say that: it includes all the good and the bad. The wild fluctuations. The long years of boredom. The sense of the self as eclipsed (by the heat, by the system, by the circumstances).

Pantone states that their Color of the Year program is, "A symbolic color selection; a color snapshot of what we see taking place in our global culture that serves as an expression of a mood and an attitude." 2017's color is Greenery, a semi-pleasant shade that I'd rather just leave you to imagine. (If it helps, Pantone describes it as "nature's neutral.") Most of the recent annual colors have also had environmentally-motivated names (Radiant Orchid, 2014; Emerald, 2013; Tangerine Tango, 2012; Honeysuckle, 2011) and those that don't are named simply (Turquoise, 2010; Blue Turquoise, 2005; True Red, 2002; Cerulean, 2000).

Color-naming is a sensitive subject. Too often it calls to mind a certain kind of power struggle: we name things not just for what we see, but how we see them. The color becomes a referent for something we want to remember, or think we know. With this color set, I'm providing an interpretation of an experience. I've tried to name these colors by saying only what I saw: the side of a house, the glaze on a tile, the sheen on a leaf, a fallen blossom. What does it mean to remove color from its source? There's a certain safety in knowing you can't tell me my red isn't "really" hibiscus.

Abstraction, like politics, can try the patience. It can be difficult to accept that some of the meaning we discover is imposed by what we see — or even worse, by how we live. A diagnosis of *chromophobia* has been closely linked to legacies of colonialism. The production of the *perfect white* (my photo backdrops, for example, come in *white*, *pure white*, and *super white*, not to mention offshoots like *eggshell*, and this doesn't even begin to touch the fantastic range of whites produced by any commercial paint company) is the eternal quest for purity — with a subtle range of names and intended uses that keep us within the lines.

If the bright color palette is foreign, somehow mysterious or inferior, what is the faded-bright? The brights traveled far during periods of serious Diaspora, but the fade seems to say we're beyond all that now. The ravages of time and weather go far beyond the control of culture, or of the paint can. Software makes it very difficult to sort things by color. This is one case where technology allows us to pretend that our world is better than it is. In reality, we sort things by color all the time.

All scientific evidence suggests that chromophobia is learned.

There are some colors I can only describe: the color of white people carrying greasy bags from Gene's while talking about their worst hangovers. The color of an old man slowly riding a powder blue bike the wrong way up Elysian Fields. The color of the abandoned house, still boarded up, across the street from a row of new renovation. The color of crustpunk dog. The color of *we didn't mean for it to be this way*. The color of faces. (Who do you see when I say that?)

I don't pretend that these colors will always be the same.

(As collected on a hot sunny day in early June 2017, on a walk through Marigny and the French Quarter with Imani Jacqueline Brown.)

Subject to change without notice.

CHAPTER EIGHT:

COMPLETE

UPON

ARRIVAL

Complete upon arrival

Do we invent the people we love?

Concluding *The Book of Everyday Instruction*,
Chapter Eight tracks the relationship between me
and various audiences over the course of producing
this project. Audience groups are divided into
four major categories, each of which I have also
"performed" as an aspect of making this work:
students, curators, writers, and artists. The
chapter focuses on the return to the self as an
essential element for understanding the pair.

Chapter Eight consists of four sentences:

> For years I followed you like a tail, and on
> happy days I wagged.

> I will be you when I have what you have.

> While away, I imagine you as different, but
> upon return I find you're just the same.

> In the end, I invented you one by one.

These four sentences are represented on
sweatshirts, in a photo series, on custom-
printed Lifesavers candy, and as a text-based
wallpaper installation.

Chapter Eight originally premiered at Spring
Break Art Fair, as part of the booth *(En)Coded
Conversations*, curated by Amanda McDonald-
Crowley.

December 2017 - January 2018

New York, NY

For years I
followed you
like a tail, and
on happy days,
I wagged.

I will be you
when I have
what you have.

While away,
I imagine you
as different,
but upon return,
I find you're
just the same.

In the end,
I invented you
one by one.

FACING PAGE: *Complete upon arrival*
as installed at the Knockdown Center, 2018

Complete upon arrival (Student), 2018.

Complete upon arrival (Curator), 2018.

Complete upon arrival (Artist), 2018.

Complete upon arrival (Writer), 2018.

while away, I imagine
you as different, but
upon return, I find
you're just the same.

In the end,
I invented you
one by one.

Exhibition continues in nearby restrooms.

PREVIOUS SPREAD: *Complete upon arrival*
as installed at the Knockdown Center, 2018
ABOVE: customized mints produced for
audience members to take.

AFTER
WORDS

Dear Chloë,

As you know, I recently made a trip to San Francisco for an art and technology conference. It was an unexpected invitation, one that I questioned because I was unsure as to how I fit into the scope of the convening. But who doesn't love a free trip to the Bay?

Everything about my travel to California was routine: the packing, the presentation preparation, the train ride to JFK. Despite the six hour flight, I still convinced myself that I would have enough energy to take public transit into San Francisco's Mission neighborhood where I would be staying for the weekend. I landed. I grabbed my bags and began to make my way to the airport's BART entrance before abruptly stopping in the middle of terminal two. As fellow travelers hurdled past me, I clumsily made my way to a bench nearby, taking deep breaths in order to calm myself.

I don't know if what I felt could be described as a panic attack, but I was certainly momentarily destabilized. Four days earlier, Nia Wilson—an 18-year-old Black woman from Oakland—was stabbed and killed by a white vigilante while traveling home on BART from a party with her older sister Lahtifa. Now, back home in Brooklyn, I still don't understand, in proper medical terms at least, what happened to my body in that moment. I had never felt that feeling before. And yet, I am simultaneously deeply aware of what it was: a striking sense of fear manifesting itself within my body.

When I first learned of Nia Wilson's death, I was scrolling through Twitter on my phone. I swallowed hard as the news became clear: murder. Her name and image was everywhere due largely to the many Black women who were amplifying the news of the attack. I swapped my phone for my computer and kept reading. I exhausted myself trying to understand the details. Where was she coming from? Where was she going? Did her murderer seek her out? Did he get away? Was her sister still alive? Why were they harmed in the first place? Sleep was difficult that night.

Most of the people in my life know that I have an extraordinary disdain for New York City's subway system. It is slow, ripe with consistent mechanical breakdowns and "planned" repairs, not accommodating to disabled passengers, and has subjected riders to a steady barrage of fare hikes since 2008. Still, I depend on this system to transport me everywhere throughout the city. Even on the late nights, during the most terrible rides, I have never felt "unsafe." I kept thinking about this as I sat in the airport waiting for my Uber. The nights when I've relied on transit to get me home at 2am because I was too broke to afford a cab. The morning commute to work, the Saturday trip to the library, returning home on any arbitrary weeknight from a talk or a movie or a concert. As Nia made her way back home, how could she have known what was coming? Who was coming.

In a recent New Yorker article about Wilson, Doreen St. Felix writes, "There is a blinkered symmetry to the way Americans have been taught to understand violence that is gendered and violence that is racialized: the victims of the former are white women; the victims of the latter are black men. The same violence, when visited upon black women, falls outside the recognizable parameters of victimhood, and thus fails to register." That is, America lacks the vocabulary to attend to the particular traumas and violences enacted upon Black women. (Here, I want to note that I am thinking of Black womanhood in the broadest of senses, i.e. young, old, disabled, able-bodied, trans women, cisgendered women, formally educated or not.) It might be better to ask: does America care for Black women? One might answer, quite simply: no.

Where can we go in order to be whole? I mean this in ways that are material and immaterial. Who keeps me fed? Who challenges me? Who do I learn from? Who will let me rest? Who keeps me safe?

In considering this letter as an invitation to reflect on *The Book of Everyday Instruction*, I cannot help but reflect, to a certain extent, on the place I currently call home. How it has held me, and how it is also, always changing. For this reason, so much of my (self) protection, how I have (self) preserved, is with and in the company of other Black women. Acknowledging this community of women as one that has cared for me is deeply political and deeply personal. I imagine this statement to be one I would have shared with you were I part of the contingency of folks you met with while working on Chapter Five. Wilson's murder jolted in me a reminder that to be a Black woman is to know that (public) safety can never be assumed within a system that hardly sees you. Though brief in nature, St. Felix's essay calls attention to the fact that there is nothing casual about Wilson's death. "It is a reflection of how this country values the lives of Black women," she writes. The places where we live define us in so many ways.

This brings me to the central question of Chapter Six: How do we share love between individuals and institutions? I see the concern of safety and preservation intimately connected to the concerns of how (social) institutions are constructed and who they ultimately serve, for whom they are built. Through my own participation in this chapter as an invited discussant, I realized the envisioning and building of such spaces first emerge from a place of intentional vulnerability which gives way to (better) language of care and healing that inform actions of care and healing. This is why I am thankful for the Black women who hold me up. That is, my body and my spirit have been taken care of within the circles of kinship I have formed. Gwendolyn Brooks reminds us: we are each other's business; we are each other's harvest; we are each other's magnitude and bond. I find this a beautiful way to think about care and love— between two people and certainly as an embodiment of an ethos of righteous structural forces. Your work has made space for this meditation. The micro and the macro.

What do we need to be safe in the places that we call home? What does our world building look like?

It is a task that, for me, is both hyper local and far reaching in its consequences, daunting, yet not impossible. It looks like Fannie Lou Hamer's Freedom Farm in Mississippi. It's the work and mission of BYP 100. It's the United Order of Tents and Dr. Josephine English. It's that infamous writing club with Toni Morrison and June Jordan and Alice Walker. It's a healthcare system in which we do not languish, a justice system which does not actively seek our imprisonment and death. It's universal pre-school. It's living wages.

It's rest.

During my car ride into San Francisco, I was not thinking about all of this, of course. It was just some time that allowed me to grieve. To momentarily thwart a real anxiety. To lift up the life of a Black woman.

Onward,

JESSICA LYNNE

I'd thought of writing this in the form of a letter, a form of faux/real 'intimacy'... à la the best thing anyone has written about me (MYSTI's "Incontinence of the Event"), à la Chloë and my dead loverboy Frank O'Hara and his "Personism" ("At last the poem is between two people instead of two pages"). Which is also to admit that I had certain preconceived ideas walking into *The Book of Everyday Instruction* at the Knockdown Center, especially knowing I was meant to write on it. I'd assumed having seen and heard various chapters and segments of chapters in advance, and having been in dialogue with the artist throughout the creation of most of The Book, that I basically got it, that I knew what my BFF was up to. I'd thought, for instance, of writing on the materiality of the exhibited objects vis-a-vis that which they document - a bit along the lines of a short text I wrote for the occasion of Chapter One's first exhibition at SPACES in Cleveland, OH. What I hadn't gleaned from the privilege of proximity to the source, I assumed I'd discern in familiar modes of reception - "seeing the show."

However, what seeing the show - the whole ensemble of the eight chapters - instead brought home was that I haven't listened carefully enough to the way Chloë says, "intimacy." Influenced by our mutual reading, by the decontextualized individual bits of the full work I'd seen, by Chloë's proximity to a world of discourse around "Social Practice," and now, in retrospect, by a certain sloppiness of familiarity on my part, I'd always heard intimacy's warmer, tender note. After sitting with the show, beyond the sunniness of its surface (more on that in a moment), I'm much more struck with a sense of exhaustion, tristesse, a feeling of rawness. For Bass (yes, the conscious shift to the proper name), as the show makes strikingly clear, intimacy is a measure — not per se of fond affection, but of affection as such. Likewise as a measure of closeness: 'closeness' only in the strict sense of proximity as a spectrum. In *The Book of Everyday Instruction*, intimacy is distance, separation — not so much ambiguous as it is aporetic.

One strand of preconception that made at least a bit of sense after the encounter with the show was my imagining Bass' work as a response to, or a corrective of, Roland Barthes' *How to Live Together* (which, down to the "trait" on proxemics, is full of nominal similarities with *The Book*). I'd imagined reading the ensembles, the pairings that orient each part of Bass' chapters, as rhythmic investigations. What I hadn't quite imagined was the degree of syncopation these encounters would contain. The presence of the world throughout *The Book*, in all chapters (a stark example: Walter Jamison's account of the racialized spatiality of segregated Greensboro in Chapter Three), ruptures any suggestion of periodicity in twoness. The author and the subject are never alone, never just together — whether infrastructurally in terms of the material provenance of an object or relationally in terms of a given mode of address. That presence of history, with all its violent inequalities, cutting through and joining all the duos of her investigation, stuttering its rhythms, is an acknowledgement of the persistent, constitutive intermingling of the normative and the "idiorhythmic" (Barthes' "utopian" notion of relations in which each may follow their own rhythm). Sure, Bass discovers idiorhythms everywhere (any of the durations of others' 'normal' activities in Chapter One, say), but what she takes this as telling us is that idiorhythms are not only not utopian, but that they also don't particularly help. Or rather, she clarifies that if one were to truly gesture toward an idiorhythmic utopia, it would mean a dissolution of the world, a vibrational polyrhythmy oscillating us toward a paradigm wholly inarticulable from where we are. Perhaps that's some of the melancholy of *The Book*'s affect? But there I go ventriloquising Chloë again.

The only trace of an approach I brought with me that led me beyond myself was the simple thought of paying attention to the forms of relation the show itself stages: how it addresses us, recognizes us, the spatial relationships its install positions us in, how it implicates our relations to it as its very subject. What struck me there was the "sunny" familiarity of its surface — a field of givens — of hospitality — modes of address that feel almost invisibly common: flowers in antique bottles (a type of arrangement also familiar in commercial display, restaurants, say), informational wall text (in an attractive font; a design element), dollar store this and that, quaintly outdated items (letter punch tags, letter board signage), a certain balance of mixed media that immediately reads as "installation," handwriting (I overhear another visitor refer to it as "girly"), hashtags (on mints). Recognize recognize recognize — and then what? What kind of a 'whole' emerges? What kind of a whole is a chapter? What kind of a whole is a 'piece' in a chapter? If every component is common, is of/in the world, what do they become together? If not wholes, nowhere, then singularities? Eminently specific entities that are internally plural. And the more I look the more I find these convolutes bumping into and against each other, distinct and yet all in relation, deferring, everywhere. Here was also the mistake of my initial assumptions: basing my reading on single moments of individual chapters. When confronted with the whole buzzing thing, the moment to moment sense of any one part is immediately broken, complicated, inflected by another. Not just in terms of the eight chapters themselves, but in every register of the piece: in the relations of the component pieces of each chapter as well as in the relations of the component "raw materials" of each piece. A chapter: constituted by, often, some form of standalone text, a performance, objects, images — all of which must be read together to constitute a singular complex body. Take, for instance, Chapter Four: the divergent media involved in the workbook, measuring performance, measuring tape object, and video are all more or less of a conceptual "piece" - but in combination with *The Glossary of Proximity Verbs*' deeply material, sensual, and ambiguous erotics, the measuring pieces shift; as do both of these elements vis-a-vis the bathroom work, a piece that double underscores the transgressive notes present throughout the chapter. Likewise one level "up": the wall text articulating the metastructure of *The Book* (the very titles of the chapters themselves): beyond its design function it reframes its referents, sets them in a particular light, casts yet another inflection of reading beyond the already vibrating differences contained in the material components of any given chapter. Even in the wall text itself, more deferral: between the title and the central question attached to it: *"Chapter Seven: Subject to change without notice.* How do we recognize an ongoing coupling in spite of change?" - if the App alone (City Palette) might not tend to be read as more than a technological amusement, tinged by the ensemble, by the title, the flags, the newsprint give-away, it's suddenly flush with a bittersweet sense of the transitory — the limits of communicability (what does the reduction of a photo to a single RGB color and its user-assigned name tell us?), of sight (an other "sees" the same site as a different reduced color), of recognition. In any given chapter we're contending with: wildly divergent and mutually cross-complicating media joined together by a poetic/informational textual framing mechanism that calibrates but also amplifies the complexities of the parts it contains. And that x8. Singularities upon singularities.

So how then to read the presence of conventions of courtesy attached to these work-complexes constituted almost exclusively by fragmentation and absence? Ironically? As a gesture of conciliation? Resignation? If the public sphere and public speech still remain deeply entangled with the problem of universalized white masculinity, High Art rationalism, and supposed "neutrality," to what public, or to what notion of a public, is Chloë Bass speaking? If Bass is not inviting us to perform a kind of "civil looking" — as in a form of looking in tune with the sensual conventions of civil society, how are we to apprehend her work? If her pieces are not objects but singularities, where exactly is "the work?" In any of the elements? In the encounters they trace? In the grammar of their presentation and combination? On the contrary it would seem that the "civility" of invitation that the entry into Bass' thought announces is a civility borne of universal fragmentation, alienation. That is, that not just the works are singularities, but we too as visitors. Perhaps Nathaniel Mackey is helpful here, from his essay, "Limbo, Dislocation, Phantom Limb: Wilson Harris and the Caribbean Occasion": "The Caribbean's brokenness participates in a larger-than-local problematic, the universal human predicament Harris calls 'cosmic frailty,' an ontological estrangement or weakness the Caribbean writer, having no historically sustained 'coherency' as insulation or defense, is in a position to confess. [...] [A] universal condition of exile." The condition of the anonymous encounter between viewer and work staged by Bass would rest on a universality such as this - one that would still be as unequally and traumatically distributed as the Western humanist variety, but without the same conception of the human.

This is also maybe a place I can try to venture a few lines on the aesthetics of social practice versus Social Practice Art. If the problem of Social Practice Art is its illustrative closeness to exemplary liberalism, liberal state art, what Bass' work makes clear to me is that this problem is deeper than surface political affinities, is rooted instead in the very notion of Art as such - in social practice's ambivalent relation to it. As Kerstin Stakemeier puts it at the beginning of her recent and hopefully soon to be translated book, Entgrenzter Formalismus, "instead of as an endangered or even lost achievement, [we] approach the modern autonomy of art as a historical disciplining of aesthetic practice" - that is, that Art as it remains hegemonically conceived is fundamentally a problem. Which would also be to say that in another thinking of an aesthetics of social practice, an aspiration would be to NOT be Art, and instead to develop the outlines of an aesthetic practice as yet unnamed and unconceived (a notion that seems nascent in social practice discourse, but never entirely disambiguated from 'the artistic'). In the meantime,

in the space of that unconceivedness, Bass' project
sits awkwardly (and more and more so as her work
is more and more seen) with both Art and Social
Practice. Too social for Art, too Art for Social
Practice, too social for the given social itself :
for those civil modes that are tentatively retained
in both "disciplines," and are retained in concert
with the grim histories of that particular civitas.

This returns me a last time to Bass' mode of address.
Instead of setting the stage for familiarity and
comfort as politeness most often does, Bass announces
the space in which she lets us know what she will and
will not do for us. It is a smile that says, "No." It
is the space in which she articulates her refusal to
take control, to tell you what to think, to look for
you, to, in a certain dramatically put sense, be "The
Artist." Which is not at all to say there is nothing
to say, nothing to read or see — what there is is
vast and infinitely specific and imbued with a rare
intelligence and sentiment. But the only way you can
see it is to take responsibility for your own seeing.
To take responsibility for yourself as another
singularity, a specific singularity bringing with it
all the historical baggage that is positionality.
Bass invites us to play a different game, one in which
neither the rules nor we are familiar. So we have to be
polite. From that Barthes book, on tact: "Tact would
mean: distance and respect, a relation that's in no
way oppressive but at the same time where there's a
real warmth of feeling. Its principle would be: not
to direct the other, other people, not to manipulate
them, to actively renounce images (the images we
have of each other), to avoid anything that might
feed the imaginary of the relation." I'm wondering
how this does or doesn't relate to some lines from
Adrian Piper's, "The Real Thing Strange": "[T]his
territory extends further into the deep regions of
the mind than the limitations of judgment, language,
intellect, or self can comfortably contain. [/] To
be at home in this place means to be comfortable
with unsynthesized intuitions: with unfamiliar
things and happenings and states and presences that
confound and silence the mind and decompose the
ego." Is the notion of art Piper is working with

here something beyond the problematics I've tried to sketch around that word, something as complex as would be necessary to identify with Bass' notion? Is Bass' work radically literalizing this sentiment of Piper's? Is Bass trying to make work that insists upon its reception only as such, as always, "at home... with unsynthesized intuitions?" How does this relate to the question Bass asks in the text she published marking the proximity of *The Book*'s opening and Piper's MoMA retrospective: "what if we accepted the provocations introduced by art as real strategies for changing our behavior or relationships?" Or, does what Piper writes a bit later in the same text, that, "no talk that talks can substitute for direct, unguarded, and sustained exposure to the intuitive presence of the artwork on terms that cannot be talked at all," suggest that Piper's position is indeed not only bound up with "Art," but likewise with its parallel notions of reception? The kind of reading that Bass' work asks of us cannot be entirely squared with a notion of the "intuitive" — the terms of the works' structure are, again, all of the world, all self-differing, all laden, unequal — they talk back. As do the plural and contradictory modes of recognition we have to mobilize into a reading not limited to the rational — a reading that insists on material, affective, and emotional literacies. Bass' work sets the givenness of her pieces' plural bodies into buzzing oscillation with the likewise plural, self-differing bodies of their receivers toward the possibility of interpretive emergence — in, as Mackey puts it, "a phantom reach beyond incompleteness."

As much time as I spent with the show, it also clearly wasn't nearly enough. Just getting to this starting point, I barely glimpsed the specific tensions and directions of the chapters on their own and overall. In this sense I couldn't be happier for the occasion of this book — that it offers another space to continue practicing this form of reading that Bass challenges us to find the outlines of within ourselves. What's striking vis-a-vis "real strategies for changing our behavior or relationships" is that after I left the show for the last time, my way of looking, of perceiving, of being in the world, was still of the show's. Waiting on that strange triangle of a corner at Grandview and Metropolitan for the B38 bus, I was transfixed by odd bits of trash carefully placed on the fence behind the bus stop in a way not unlike my experience of the show. Here too, an utterance of anonymous relation, a document of an encounter as a means to shift us in our encounter with it — another aesthetic practice beyond Art. I thought to take a picture for City Palette, but my phone was dead.

BILL DIETZ

BOOK AS OBJECT, BOOK AS EXERCISE, BOOK AS QUESTION: THE BOOK OF THE BOOK OF EVERYDAY INSTRUCTION AND THE OPERATING SYSTEM AS CONDUIT

Back in 2012, when I first met and started collaborating with Chloë Bass, the Operating System was in its pupa stage, gestating within a beta test version as *Exit Strata*, becoming itself. It was only beginning to be clear to me what it could fully mean to call an arts/education/ justice organization-that-publishes "a question, not an answer," an idea that's been central to our mission from day one.

What I hoped that the organization could be and do was not fixed, but some objectives were clear from the start: support work that-also-questions; build resources, tools, blueprints, and models for others; get work into the archive that resists easy acceptance/ support / categorization and might otherwise be lost; humanize and make visible the bodies and narratives behind creative practice, and actively open conversation about the systems within which this work and these bodies interface.

Which means that when I met Chloë and became familiar with her work, I was immediately drawn to another practitioner whose process was decisively question driven: whose practice was so clearly (and without apology) about exploring the intimate, familiar yet deeply foreign spaces within and between ourselves and each other. At the time, she was working on *The Bureau of Self-Recognition*, and described her intentions with this rigorous, investigatory project as "looking to build a kind of exploratory structure that de-emphasizes success in product for consistency of process."

The project was a natural match for our online *Field Notes* series, which I had developed earlier in 2012 out of a desire to have intimate conversations and "behind the curtain" exposure to creative practice. *Field Notes* seeks to celebrate and validate the living of a creative life, of engaging in a process of seeking and making, over more visible models of "success." I also hope to foster conversations with, and give a platform to, those who are open to engaging transparently with the social and cultural institutions and systems that made this approach to creative practice as a life-choice seem so impossible, unwise, even irresponsible.

Chloë's work with the *Bureau* already dismissed any illusion of a "line" between private and visible creative practice, inward-vs-public facing investigation. The goals of the *Field Notes* series was already folded into her process, so there we began a series within a series, "Consultations with the Bureau of Self Recognition." Work from this series would then appear in the print volume that came out around that time, as well as in the *Exhibit A: Re/Presentation and Re/Production* show which I curated not long after, drawing from the work of several OS contributors.

As the OS grew, my own creative practice took a curious turn: through the combination of the creative questions I had about the world, my scholarly work in the social sciences, and the ways in which my conceptual practice played with official forms, branding, identity, book making, graphic design, and texts. I saw that these combined efforts and thought streams could play together at a meta-scale: *what did it mean to hold the space of the page, and the Web, for the questions I had about the world? And, how could publishing be a continuous act of resistance, if that page-space continued to be held open for others dedicated to questions?* The publishing arm of the OS began its exponential growth once that potential became clear, and from the moment we began, I was committed to continuing our relationship with the practitioners who'd been there in the beginning, and to call out to others doing the work.

The value of the book-as-object is immensely rich as well as culturally complicated. Chloë, too, has continuously engaged with and explored the page-space, and in conversation with this value, throughout her projects over the years: *The Bureau of Self-Recognition* culminated in a hardcover, special edition monograph, and many of the chapters of *The Book of Everyday Instruction* in their original formulations/presentations included printed booklets, interventive wall texts, and hand-held text-driven objects.

When Chloë first came to me (several years ago now) with the idea of publishing the book of *The Book of Everyday Instruction*, I agreed without hesitation--but also with the awareness (confirmed by now having completed the task) that it would be a beautiful challenge to collaborate on a book-object with a fellow artist so resolutely aware of visual identity that I cannot think of her work or personal communications without very specific fonts being present.

My task was to create a book concept that drew from and on Chloë's visual language while clearly designing an object at once unique from, yet also representative of, the project itself. The design scheme plays on the utilitarian, quotidian nature of the work and its Everyday materials, and the book has been produced in an accessible, soft-cover, more affordable version, sized perhaps less as an art book than as a manual, as a *Book of Instruction* might indeed be.

Too frequently with creative practice we see work made for everyone getting repackaged through performative form and presentation into a class-driven, elitist product--so concerned are we with perception of value through these means. Instead, as I often do with OS texts, the Book has a faux-fabric cover, faux-labelling throughout, nods to other strategies and processes of making and investigation, as well as to how value is built and signalled through design. By gesturing to instead of reproducing, I hope the book can remain truer to its much greater absolute value as a human object, rather than a cultural fetish--all the while, I suppose, fetishizing itself.

As in all OS books, the book of The Book of Everyday Instruction wants to be a question: *what can a book be and do?* In this particular case, a secondary question is raised: *how can we produce value and inclusive access for all in a monograph when a monograph is such a signifier of divisory value and status?*

It's been a privilege to work closely with Chloë for over a year asking these critical questions in relationship to this project specifically, and so too in relationship to creative practice--and to creative practice's ongoing intersections with the making of public objects of consumption.

I believe that moving work into the printed archive is urgent and necessary, especially in this era of born digital media. I hope that through its making, this book helps ensure that this artist, and the critical questions of *her* making, make their way into infinite numbers of hands and minds both now and in the future.

If nothing else I am certain that in this small way, we can begin to rupture the firmament.

ELAE [Lynne DeSilva-Johnson]
Brooklyn, 2018

ACKNOWLEDGEMENTS

In its process, this project has been supported, funded, and presented by so many institutions, listed here in roughly chronological order:

SPACES, Salisbury University, Eyebeam, Upfor Gallery, Elsewhere (with outside support from ArtPlace America and the National Folk Festival), Lower Manhattan Cultural Council, the Museum of Modern Art, the Goethe-Institut, Cooper Union, the School of Visual Arts, the Rema Hort Mann Foundation, the Pulitzer Arts Foundation, the Luminary, BRIC, the Weeksville Heritage Center, CUE Art Foundation, Franklin Street Works, Tiger Strikes Asteroid NY, Antenna, the Difference and Media Project at Bard College, the Design Studio for Social Intervention, the Center for Book Arts, Triangle Arts Association, Independent Curators International, Washington and Lee University's Staniar Gallery, the Knockdown Center, and of course my home institution of Queens College, CUNY.

Portions of this text have been previously published on *Arts.Black* and the *Living Maps Review*. Other portions are being published simultaneously by Independent Curators International.

The photos on page 110 have been reprinted with the permission of the Museum of Modern Art, and were shot by Manuel Molina Martagon. The photo spread on pages 112 - 113 has been reprinted with the permission of The Kitchen, and was shot by Naima Green.

I'd like to state my awe and enthusiasm for the work of photographer Kalaija Mallery, who took many of the installation shots of the *Chloë Bass: The Book of Everyday Instruction* exhibit at the Knockdown Center, as well as the "product" photos staged in my studio; and designer/publisher extraordinaire [ELÆ]Lynne DeSilva-Johnson. You represent me as the classy person I want to be.

Since 2015, I've talked about this project with perhaps too many people to count (thank you), but I want to extend special appreciation to Bill Dietz, Jessica Lynne, Alexis Wilkinson, Doug Ashford, Naeem Mohaiemen, George Scheer, Christina Vassallo, Bruce Edwards, Tiona McClodden, Caroline Woolard, Jillian Steinhauer, Tara and David Gladden, James and Brea McAnally, Jennifer Baker, Kristin Fleischmann-Brewer, Bob Snead, Imani Jacqueline Brown, Ron Bechet, David Xu Borgonjon, Maria del Carmen Carrion, Terri Smith, Alethea Rockwell, Clover Archer, Clarinda Mac Low, Amanda McDonald-Crowley, Mollie Eisenberg, Sally Szwed, and my parents, Erica Mapp and Alan Bass: you've all been partners to me in your own ways.

ABOUT THE ARTIST

Chloë Bass is a multiform conceptual artist working in performance, situation, conversation, publication, and installation. Her work uses daily life as a site of deep research to address scales of intimacy: where patterns hold and break as group sizes expand. She began her work with a focus on the individual (*The Bureau of Self-Recognition*, 2011 — 2013), has recently concluded a study of pairs (*The Book of Everyday Instruction*, 2015 — 2017), is currently observing immediate families (*Obligation To Others Holds Me In My Place*, 2018 - 2020), and will continue to scale up gradually until she's working at the scale of the metropolis. Chloë has held numerous fellowships and residencies; 2018's include a residency at Denniston Hill, the Recess Analog Artist-in-Residence, and a BRIC Media Arts Fellowship. Her projects have appeared nationally and internationally, including recent exhibits at the Knockdown Center, the Kitchen, the Brooklyn Museum, CUE Art Foundation, Elizabeth Foundation for the Arts Project Space, The Southeastern Center for Contemporary Art, the James Gallery, and elsewhere. Reviews, mentions of, and interviews about her work have appeared in *Artforum*, *The New York Times*, *Hyperallergic*, *The Brooklyn Rail*, *BOMB*, *Temporary Art Review*, and *Artnews* among others. Her short-form writing has been published on *Hyperallergic*, *Arts.Black,* and *the Walker Reader,* as well as in the *Living and Sustaining a Creative Life* series, edited by Sharon Louden, and in Paper Monument's recent book *As radical, As Mother, As Salad, As Shelter, What Should Art Institutions Do Now?* She has a chapbook, *#sky #nofilter*, forthcoming from DoubleCross Press. A native New Yorker, Chloë lives and works in Brooklyn and is an Assistant Professor of Art at Queens College, CUNY, where she co-runs Social Practice Queens with Gregory Sholette. You can learn more about her at chloebass.com.

2015

May
The Book of Everyday Instruction, Chapter One: you+me together.
SPACES, Cleveland, Ohio.

September
*A person may be unaware of being photographed in a variety of
situations* shown as part of *Eyebeam in Objects,* Upfor Gallery,
Portland, Oregon.

October
*The Book of Everyday Instruction, Chapter Two: Things I've seen
people do lately.* Salisbury University, Salisbury, Maryland.

2016

April
*The Book of Everyday Instruction, Chapter Three: We walk the world
two by two.* Permanent installation debut, Elsewhere, Greensboro,
North Carolina.

*The Book of Everyday Instruction, Chapter Four: It's amazing
we don't have more fights. A Field Guide to Spatial Intimacy*
workshop, The Museum of Modern Art.

June
A Field Guide to Spatial Intimacy workshop presented as part of
The Goethe Institut's Kultursymposium Weimar, Germany.

September
*I put these words in the bathroom because the bathroom is a place
where people read.* Permanent installation initiated for *To A
Point,* SVA Curatorial Practice Program, New York.

October
*The Book of Everyday Instruction, Chapter Five: Protect &
Preserve.* Lecture performance and book launch, St. Louis Small
Press Expo, the Pulitzer Foundation, St. Louis, Missouri.

A Field Guide to Spatial Intimacy displayed as part of *WOUND,* The
Cooper Union, New York.

November
The Book of Everyday Instruction, Chapter One: you+me together
shown as part of *Once More, With Feeling,* EFA Project Space, New
York.

The Book of Everyday Instruction, Chapter Two: Things I've seen people do lately shown as part of the BRIC Biennial, Weeksville Heritage Center, Brooklyn, New York.

December
The Book of Everyday Instruction, Chapter Five: Protect & Preserve lecture performance at Weeksville Heritage Center.

January
The Book of Everyday Instruction, Chapter Six: What is shared, what is offered.
- * *Maintenance* shown as part of *Love Action Art Lounge*, Franklin Street Works, Stamford, Connecticut.
- * *The Four Phases of Love* shown as part of The Visible Hand, CUE Art Foundation, New York.

February
Couples Counseling for Artists and Institutions workshop, CUE Art Foundation.

What is shared, what is offered conversation series Guest #1 (Doug Ashford), Independent Curators International.

The Book of Everyday Instruction, Chapter Three: We walk the world two by two shown as part of *x≈y: An Act of Translation* at Tiger Strikes Asteroid, New York.

March
Couples Counseling For People and Blackness, keynote presentation and workshop for *Black Art Is, Black Art Ain't*, Design Studio For Social Intervention, Boston, Massachusetts.

April
Couples Counseling For People and Blackness, keynote presentation and workshop for *The Teach In*, presented by the Difference and Media Project, Bard College, Annendale-on-Hudson, New York.

June
What is shared, what is offered conversation series Guest #2 (Bill Dietz), Independent Curators International.

September
What is shared, what is offered conversation series Guest #3 (Tiona Nekkia McClodden), Independent Curators International.

October
A Field Guide to Spatial Intimacy workshop at *Teaching Social Practice* conference, University of Massachusetts Dartmouth, New Bedford, Massachusetts.

November
The Book of Everyday Instruction, Chapter Seven: Subject to change without notice, City Palette app debut and public bus ad campaign with Antenna, New Orleans, Louisiana.

What is shared, what is offered conversation series Guest #4 (Lisi Raskin), Independent Curators International.

2018

January
The Book of Everyday Instruction. Staniar Gallery, Washington & Lee University.

The Book of Everyday Instruction, Chapter Four: It's amazing we don't have more fights. A Glossary of Proximity Verbs shown as part of *predicated.*, The Kitchen, New York.

February
What is shared, what is offered conversation series Guest #5 (Jessica Lynne), Independent Curators International.

March
The Book of Everyday Instruction, Chapter Eight: Complete upon arrival shown at Spring/Break Art Fair, as part of *(En)coded Conversations*.

April
Chloë Bass: The Book of Everyday Instruction. The Knockdown Center, Queens, New York, April 2018. This exhibition included all major events from the project: *A Field Guide to Spatial Intimacy* workshop, the *Couples Counseling for Artists and Institutions* workshop, and the *Protect & Preserve* lecture performance.

August
The Book of Everyday Instruction, Chapter One: you+me together shown as part of *What We Make*, Ross Art Museum, Ohio Wesleyan University.

September
The Four Phases of Love shown at Temple Contemporary, Philadelphia, Pennsylvania.

This list is complete as of this book's publication. As time goes on, it will continue to grow.

The Operating System uses the language "print document" to differentiate from the book-object as part of our mission to distinguish the act of documentation-in-book-FORM from the act of publishing as a backwards-facing replication of the book's agentive *role* as it may have appeared the last several centuries of its history. Ultimately, I approach the book as TECHNOLOGY: one of a variety of printed documents (in this case, bound*) that humans have invented and in turn used to archive and disseminate ideas, beliefs, stories, and other evidence of production.*

Ownership and use of printing presses and access to (or restriction of) printed materials has long been a site of struggle, related in many ways to revolutionary activity and the fight for civil rights and free speech all over the world. While (in many countries) the contemporary quotidian landscape has indeed drastically shifted in its access to platforms for sharing information and in the widespread ability to "publish" digitally, even with extremely limited resources, the importance of publication on physical media has not diminished. In fact, this may be the most critical time in recent history for activist groups, artists, and others to insist upon learning, establishing, and encouraging personal and community documentation practices. Hear me out.

With The OS's print endeavors I wanted to open up a conversation about this: the ultimately radical, transgressive act of creating PRINT /DOCUMENTATION in the digital age. It's a question of the archive, and of history: who gets to tell the story, and what evidence of our life, our behaviors, our experiences are we leaving behind? We can know little to nothing about the future into which we're leaving an unprecedentedly digital document trail — but we can be assured that publications, government agencies, museums, schools, and other institutional powers that be will continue to leave BOTH a digital and print version of their production for the official record. Will we?

As a (rogue) anthropologist and long time academic, I can easily pull up many accounts about how lives, behaviors, experiences..., how THE STORY of a time or place was pieced together using the deep study of correspondence, notebooks, and other physical documents which are no longer the norm in many lives and practices. As we move our creative behaviors towards digital note taking, and even audio and video, what can we predict about future technology that is in any way assuring that our stories will be accurately told – or told at all? How will we leave these things for the record?

In these documents we say:
WE WERE HERE, WE EXISTED, WE HAVE A DIFFERENT STORY

- Elæ [Lynne DeSilva-Johnson], Founder/Creative Director
THE OPERATING SYSTEM

Ark Hive - Marthe Reed
I Made for You a New Machine and All it Does is Hope - Richard Lucyshyn
Illusory Borders - Heidi Reszies
A Year of Misreading the Wildcats - Orchid Tierney
We Are Never The Victims - Timothy DuWhite
Of Color: Poets' Ways of Making | An Anthology of Essays on Transformative Poetics -
Amanda Galvan Huynh & Luisa A. Igloria, Editors

KIN(D)* Texts and Projects

A Bony Framework for the Tangible Universe - D. Allen
Opera on TV - James Brunton
Hall of Waters - Berry Grass
Transitional Object - Adrian Silbernagel

Glossarium: Unsilenced Texts and Translations

Śnienie / Dreaming - Marta Zelwan/Krystyna Sakowicz, (Poland, trans. Victoria Miluch)
Alparegho: Pareil-À-Rien / Alparegho, Like Nothing Else - Hélène Sanguinetti
(France, trans. Ann Cefola)
High Tide Of The Eyes - Bijan Elahi (Farsi-English/dual-language, trans. Rebecca Ruth
Gould and Kayvan Tahmasebian)
In the Drying Shed of Souls: Poetry from Cuba's Generation Zero
(Katherine Hedeen and Víctor Rodríguez Núñez, translators/editors)
Street Gloss - Brent Armendinger with translations for Alejandro Méndez, Mercedes
Roffé, Fabián Casas, Diana Bellessi, and Néstor Perlongher (Argentina)
Operation on a Malignant Body - Sergio Loo (Mexico, trans. Will Stockton)
Are There Copper Pipes in Heaven - Katrin Ottarsdóttir
(Faroe Islands, trans. Matthew Landrum)

Print::Document Chapbook Series (7th Annual)

Vela. - Knar Gavin
[零] A Phantom Zero - Ryu Ando
RE: Verses - Kristina Darling and Chris Campanioni
Don't Be Scared - Magdalena Zurawski

Digital Chapbook Series (2019)

The American Policy Player's Guide and Dream Book - Rachel Zolf
Flight of the Mothman - Gyasi Hall
Mass Transitions - Sue Landers
The George Oppen Memorial BBQ - Eric Benick

An Absence So Great and Spontaneous It Is Evidence of Light - Anne Gorrick
The Book of Everyday Instruction - Chloë Bass
Executive Orders Vol. II - a collaboration with the Organism for Poetic Research
One More Revolution - Andrea Mazzariello
The Suitcase Tree - Filip Marinovich
Chlorosis - Michael Flatt and Derrick Mund
Sussuros a Mi Padre - Erick Sáenz
Sharing Plastic - Blake Nemec
In Corpore Sano : Creative Practice and the Challenged Body [Anthology]
Abandoners - Lesley Ann Wheeler
Jazzercise is a Language - Gabriel Ojeda-Sague
Born Again - Ivy Johnson
Attendance - Rocío Carlos and Rachel McLeod Kaminer
Singing for Nothing - Wally Swist
The Ways of the Monster - Jay Besemer
Walking Away From Explosions in Slow Motion - Gregory Crosby
Field Guide to Autobiography - Melissa Eleftherion

Glossarium: Unsilenced Texts and Translations

The Book of Sounds - Mehdi Navid (Farsi dual language, trans. Tina Rahimi
Kawsay: The Flame of the Jungle - María Vázquez Valdez (Mexico, trans. Margaret Randall)
Return Trip / Viaje Al Regreso - Israel Dominguez; (Cuba, trans. Margaret Randall)

Want-catcher - Adra Raine
We, The Monstrous - Mark DuCharme;
Greater Grave - Jacq Greyja
Needles of Itching Feathers - Jared Schickling

for our full catalog please visit:
https://squareup.com/store/the-operating-system/

deeply discounted Book of the Month and Chapbook Series subscriptions
are a great way to support the OS's projects and publications!
sign up at: http://www.theoperatingsystem.org/subscribe-join/

DOC U MENT
/däkyəmənt/

First meant "instruction" or "evidence," whether written or not.

noun - a piece of written, printed, or electronic matter that provides information or evidence or that serves as an official record
verb - record (something) in written, photographic, or other form
synonyms - paper - deed - record - writing - act - instrument

[*Middle English, precept, from Old French, from Latin documentum, example, proof, from docre, to teach; see dek- in Indo-European roots.*]

Who is responsible for the manufacture of value?

Based on what supercilious ontology have we landed in a space
where we vie against other creative people in vain pursuit
of the fleeting credibilities of the scarcity economy, rather than
freely collaborating and sharing openly with each other
in ecstatic celebration of MAKING?

While we understand and acknowledge the economic pressures and fear-mongering that
threatens to dominate and crush the creative impulse, we also believe that
now more than ever we have the tools to relinquish agency via cooperative means,
fueled by the fires of the Open Source Movement.

**Looking out across the invisible vistas of that rhizomatic parallel country
we can begin to see our community beyond constraints,
in the place where intention meets
resilient, proactive, collaborative organization.**

Here is a document born of that belief, sown purely of imagination and will.
When we document we assert. We print to make real, to reify our being there.
When we do so with mindful intention to address our process,
to open our work to others, to create beauty in words in space,
to respect and acknowledge the strength of the page
we now hold physical, a thing in our hand,
we remind ourselves that, like Dorothy:
we had the power all along, my dears.

THE PRINT! DOCUMENT SERIES
is a project of
the trouble with bartleby
in collaboration with
the operating system

While away,
I imagine you
as different,
but upon return,
I find you're
just the same.

In the end,
I invented you
one by one.

CPSIA information can be obtained
at www.ICGtesting.com
Printed in the USA
BVHW061623210119
538286BV00001B/94/P